Teaching & Coaching

LAWN TENNIS

Teaching & Coaching
LAWN TENNIS

A. Wallis Myers, C.B.E.

SPORTS PUBLICATION

7/26, Ground Floor, Ansari Road, Darya Ganj,
New Delhi-110 002. Ph.: (O) 55749511, 55257538
(M) 9868028838 (R) 27562163

Published by:

SPORTS PUBLICATION
H.O.: 7/26, Ground Floor, Ansari Road,
Darya Ganj, New Delhi-110 002.
B.O. C-13, Rose Apartment, Sector-14 Extn.,
Rohini, Delhi-110 085.
Ph. : (O) 55749511, 55257538 (R) 27562163, (M) 9868028838
E-mail: *ektathani@hotmail.com*
Website : www.sportspublication.trade-india.com

First Published 2006

I.S.B.N. – 81-7879-267-2

PRINTED IN INDIA 2006

Laser Typeset by:

JAIN MEDIA GRAPHICS, Delhi-110035. Ph.: 27190244

Printed by:

CHAWLA OFFSET PRINTERS, Delhi-110052

Price Rs. 150/-

CHAPTER
O N E

THE PASTIME OF ALL PEOPLES

LAWN TENNIS
ITS PRINCIPLES & PRACTICE

CHAPTER ONE

THE PASTIME OF ALL PEOPLES

THE Pastime of all Peoples! It is a bold and sweeping claim, yet justified by a survey of relative facts. Lawn tennis, of buried or at any rate obscure origin, barely out of its fragile teens at the beginning of the twentieth century, struggling for life against the vested interests of ancient and conservative rivals, ever the sport of prejudice, has developed into a world game unrestricted in expansion by frontier, language, climate, or sex.

In mid-Victorian times it was unknown. In the early 'seventies a few scattered disciples of rackets and tennis (the latter a forbear from which it derived its name), more by accident than by design, experimented on their home lawns with a game so unpretentious and apparently so transitory that all its implements, except the court and the players, were contained in a portable box. A toy, in fact!

> " *Those that with haste will make a mighty fire*
> *Begin it with weak straws.*"

None of those late Victorian pioneers, pegging out an hour-glass-shaped court on a lawn hitherto sacred to croquet and crinolines, and bisecting their claim with a high net, supported by guy ropes attached to posts and sagging in the centre, could have realised the touchstone they were applying to a world game. The seed sown on those private lawns of England was to fructify beyond the dreams of its casual planters. Their abbreviated courts were to multiply into an illimitable province. A garden diversion, spurned by many men of vigour and intelligence, derided by the few newspapers which deigned to notice its arrival, was to become, in little more than a generation, the most popular ball game in the civilised world. Only the players, exercising their crude art in turn, watched the first games of lawn tennis ; in less than half a century the stands at Wimbledon were to prove inadequate to accommodate the thousands anxious to witness championship matches. And the competitors would represent as many as thirty different countries. Behind them, in near or distant lands, waiting for the results to arrive, would be other thousands of club and local adherents. Neither sex, race, nor class would divide these disciples ; they would all be units in a great and cosmopolitan family.

The greater part of them would never have played on the game's original surface. Only a few of the countries which now pursue lawn tennis have turf courts. Europe has none except in Britain and Ireland. America has none west of Chicago. Those in California are of cement. India has its grass courts ; these are foreign to Japan. Australia and New Zealand utilise turf ; South Africa employs ant-heap ; the courts of South America are mineral-made. The favoured courts in Scandinavia are covered and of wood.

The world has embraced lawn tennis without embracing its original surface. Thereby its cosmic power is illustrated. The highest art of the game, its refinements of foot and ball work and its subtleties of spin, may still be expressed on the best turf court ; the fact remains that more lawn tennis is played on non-turf floors, and that those who have won the highest honours in the last decade, even on a grass surface, have learnt and developed their game on an artificial plane. Occasion will be found later on to discuss this theme in relation to strokes and strategy. Here the general point is made that lawn tennis needed the wider environment of world acceptance before its virtues could be adapted, in varying degree, to the social conditions of individual States. Its progress was not sweeping, like that of wireless telegraphy ; in other countries besides England it had to dissolve prejudice. But the seed, wherever it was dropped, fell on fertile soil ; the game created its own court and reconciled its pursuit to every new environment.

The British authors of lawn tennis have, therefore, much to their credit. They founded a pastime which permitted men and women of all nationalities to meet in friendly competition under a common code of rules. By its popular vogue and catholicity the game provided a medium for physical and mental expression that was satisfying both to the individual and to the patriot. "Words but direct, example must allure," says Stirling. The athletic emancipation of women has been hastened and nourished by lawn tennis, a game happy in its scope for industry, movement, and grace.

No invention could have been better timed. It arrived to give society of either sex not only exercise and health, but, as its cult developed, an art through which national characteristics could be exploited. The lawn tennis court became an international arena ; the language of the court assumed the power and utility of Esperanto ; frontiers melted before the game ; the pride of race and individuality was stimulated at the same time.

Lawn tennis was first pursued on private English lawns by middle-aged people. Its original disciples, as I have said, had been addicted to rackets and real tennis, the royal and ancient game. They were men of part or whole leisure, and their womenfolk, praising Providence for providing an outdoor exercise more violent than croquet, found an athletic status equal to that of their lords. Small wonder they embraced it, first with curiosity and then with devotion. Croquet mallets were flung down, domestic lawns were bisected by nets ; in some cases, where Nature interfered, noble oaks and elms were sacrificed.

Lawn tennis spread, not with the violence and speed of the prairie fire, but gently and insidiously, like influenza. It was a social diversion, frequently lampooned in *Punch*, never taken seriously by those who did not pursue it, never visualised as a world sport by those who did. Its first adherents were men of sedate habits and of muscles trained for games with standardised and fixed styles. The feet were anchored for the service, the face of the racket was little more than half the size of the modern weapon, the net was almost U-shaped, the balls were not always covered with cloth, the staple stroke was a slice as in tennis, and the side-line drive was unknown. The game was grafted on to ancient games by a conservative people. The prophets of the 'seventies might have seen in this very fact the germ of greatness ; it was not detected until the Renshaw twins, with youth and supple limbs at their command, revealed the potentialities of a vigorous competitive art.

The Renshaw brothers were the real fathers of lawn tennis as we know it to-day, and had they not accepted the faith, making converts by their personality and other champions by their example, it is conceivable that the pastime would have died a natural death, or, at any rate, like the original net, have been in suspended animation. One may note in passing that the twins developed their art, not on a turf surface, but on a covered floor of tar asphalt. The fact was significant. The original nursery of the game in England was a private lawn, frequently mossy, generally

Fig. 1.

WILLIAM & ERNEST RENSHAW.
From a contemporary Journal.

clotted in the matter of grass roots ; well mown, of course, but more like a Turkey carpet than the firm, resilient plane on which the modern game has been bred. The motto of the aboriginals was "Safety First" ; they had to dig the ball out of the ground. The gardener's ideal of a lawn tennis court in the 'eighties—and the first championship meetings at Wimbledon embraced it—was that honoured in the college quadrangles at Cambridge. When invading sight-seers asked for the recipe the answer would be, "Mow and roll daily for three hundred years."

The English style was founded on such a surface; it may be said to have been handicapped by it ever since. Half a century ago the prevailing habit was to hit the ball from corner to corner—an almost interminable exchange; and for this custom the nature of the surface and the uneven height of the net was the main cause. Ireland attained distinction because her countrymen—then, as now, iconoclastic—invented a running drive, a kind of forcing shot off a low ball. 'Turf' is a dialect word for peat, and many

Fig. 2.

A GLADIATOR OF THE 'EIGHTIES.
H. F. Lawford, winner of the Singles Championship, 1887.
From the *Graphic*.

a court resembled an Irish bog. It was by perfecting a slow running drive that W. J. Hamilton, one of the brilliant Dublin group, won both the English and the Irish Championship, and it was another Irishman, J. C. Parke, whose powers of mobility on a wet court, developed on the Rugby football field, made him famous both in England and in Australia. Parke was not a great player in the classical sense; his service was unprovocative; he had limitations as a volleyer. Leinster gave him his character; a stout arm and a stout heart won him his victories.

Had there been no other surface but turf on which to pursue lawn tennis its career must have been cabined and confined. The game would never have become a world pastime, for the reason that grass courts are unknown in most countries. And it was almost an accident which first introduced the game into France. The original outdoor court was constructed of a binding sand, extracted from the Esterel Mountains, a beautiful feature of the Côte d'Azur. It was laid down in the garden of the Hôtel Beau Site, Cannes, in the early 'eighties in order that the

A CHAMPIONSHIP COMPETITOR IN 1884.

Renshaw brothers, wintering abroad, might pursue their hobby. This court has become famous, not only by virtue of its history, but because almost every champion, including several from America, has played on it. After Cannes came other courts of a similar substance on the Riviera. The game had already been practised on covered courts in Paris ; other capitals met a growing demand. Stockholm, illustrating Swedish enterprise, built a flock of covered courts, installing artificial light to defy the winter.

It was natural that continental players should develop at a greater speed than those from England, where climate and surface checked incubation. For nearly a decade no really first-class player from France emerged, and the British player of first-class rank could generally anticipate victory at the summer tournaments which he visited.

This ascendancy, appearing to ignore the incidence of surface, was only temporary. It was due partly to the colonising faculty of the British, permitting them to impose their coolness and phlegm in a new environment, and partly to the relative inexperience of their opponents. The strokes of Max Decugis and André Gobert were more fluent and pleasing to the eye than those of men who beat them at first in actual match play ; the will to win, dominant in the visitor, was absent. As soon as it was cultivated —and its growth was essential—the tables were turned. The benefits of surface, of quicker footwork, of a firm eye, were realised. The Dohertys, with their outstanding genius, could always beat the best Frenchmen, Germans, or Belgians of their epoch, just as they beat, save on one or two memorable occasions, the best Americans. But the Dohertys had classical strokes and a temperament far above the average. They stood out in their era just as the Renshaws stood out before them and Mlle Lenglen and W. T. Tilden after them. They betrayed national characteristics as other champions betrayed them, but they were thrown up, almost in splendid isolation, by the evolution of time.

No one country can claim or can expect a monopoly of such phenomena. It might be assumed that either France, which produced Suzanne Lenglen, or America, which provided Helen Wills [afterwards Mrs. F. S. Moody], would have supplied successors or antitypes to these fine stroke players. Both inspired the youth of their respective countries ; they fired a trail among the girlhood of Europe and America and of countries beyond which is still blazing ; and if one became a professional and the other remained an amateur the value of their personalities in developing women's play cannot be overestimated. And yet, strange to say, neither France nor America produced a player who could be regarded as a greater artist than either of these two.

The distinction fell on Spain. Señorita Elia de Alvarez, the most brilliant exponent of the modern game, combined with grace of movement a vigorous stroke and an intuitive skill which made her a most fascinating player to watch. Though born of Spanish parents she had spent nearly all her life outside Spain—in Italy, France, Germany, Switzerland, and England, migrating from place to place with her parents. This movement had nourished her versatility; she was adept at languages and at many other sports besides lawn tennis. It also deepened her character; she would have been much less an artist if she had spent her life in Spain. National traits—fluency of movement, impetuosity, dignity of carriage—were visible. But she developed mentally in excess of her sisters because of her contact with the outer world; not otherwise would she have attained the self-reliance which was at once a feature and a force in her lawn tennis.

CHAPTER
TWO

EVOLUTION AND INTERNATIONAL TRAITS

CHAPTER TWO

EVOLUTION AND INTERNATIONAL TRAITS

§ I

DURING the first half-century of lawn tennis the sceptre of power may be said to have passed to five countries in turn. It may not be unprofitable to note these cycles in sequence and to examine their causes. England was naturally pre-eminent in the first epoch. Her natives had founded the game, competition from outside was limited and fugitive ; laurels were collected more or less automatically. But the strokes and strategy of the Englishmen had been developed and intensified by international matches with Ireland. When the Renshaws retired, the English group surrounding them missed their inspiration, and since most of their members were nearing middle-age the standard of play was inclined to fall. Irish enterprise and audacity revived it, and Dublin provided in Joshua Pim a champion whose game had the hall-mark of genius.

The matches for the championship at Wimbledon between Pim and Wilfred Baddeley crystallised two schools—the cautious, calculating methods of the Englishman and the robust, adventurous, intuitive style of the Irishman. The latter did not always prevail, but its greater brilliance was undeniable, and when Pim was at his best he was virtually unplayable. It is scarcely exaggerating to say that he could hit a coin placed anywhere on the court. When America saw Dr. Pim in the early Davis Cup matches, he had emerged from retirement and was but a shadow of the real champion. Both Pim and Baddeley were all-court players ; they had absorbed the art of the Renshaws, though neither had the rapidity of execution of William nor the meticulous accuracy of Ernest.

Evolution had been at work steadily. The Renshaws had to create strokes—there had been none to guide them ; their successors got the benefit of precedent and the encouragement of example. As the Renshaws began

England's supremacy, so the reign of the Dohertys ended it. These famous brothers may have lacked the fire and physique of some of their predecessors and some of their successors, but they resisted all-comers for ten years. An occasional defeat in the doubles at Wimbledon only served to emphasise the volume of their triumphs. They were the "Princes Charming" of the lawn tennis court, and the grace of their deportment and the serenity of their temper have never been equalled. Yet, perfect stylists as they were, with no vulnerable chink in their armour, it may be doubted whether the increased pace and tension of tennis in after years would not have imposed their physique to an insupportable strain. It is true that they won matches in the heat and tumult of America against America's picked men, but the American players at the beginning of the century were not so versatile in attack nor so powerful in service and drive as their successors of the next decade.

It has been said that, given present-day conditions, the Dohertys would have mastered them just as they mastered the googly service of Dwight Davis and Holcombe Ward when they first encountered it. The game, however, has moved forward with each succeeding decade. The advance may not be detected as and when it occurs; the faithful historian, in looking back, is conscious of it. In women's play progress was well-nigh revolutionary even within a couple of decades. The champions of the past, could they be restored at their best, would find the champion of the present in a class above them. Improved equipment, changes in dress, greater opportunities for practice, the stimulant of publicity, have all promoted progress. It is not suggested, of course, that the champions of the past, given the same assets, would not have exploited them to equal—and possibly in some cases greater—advantage. For in Miss L. Dod, to name only one player, Wimbledon had a youthful champion, younger than, and as versatile as, Mlle Lenglen, who came thirty-two years after her. Genius will shine in any age, but more brightly in an age when the flame is fed.

Australasia was the third country to furnish a world's champion. Norman Brookes for two years and Anthony Wilding for four won the title at Wimbledon, and, between them, these two in alliance carried off the Davis Cup. The first was an artist, unmatched in volleying skill, the second an athlete, wielding drives sustained in vigour by inexhaustible stamina. Both possessed the confidence and courage indigenous to their respective lands, and although they differed as much in personality as in the methods of their play, they enjoyed the common heritage of forceful character.

Norman Brookes also had the asset of surprise attack. Britons and Americans were in the lead ; no other country was deemed ripe enough to dispute their claim. Norman Brookes was the " dark horse " of 1905. His destructive service and magical volleying dominated Wimbledon of that year ; his path to the title was only checked by H. L. Doherty, who stood out of the championship until the challenge round. When Brookes returned to England two years later his service was strengthened materially. A great English driver, S. H. Smith, had demonstrated that a break delivery, however sinister, could be smothered at birth if the proper weapon was employed. The Brookes of 1907 had added length and pace to his service, qualities which strengthened his complementary volleying and added to the number of his victims.

Wilding's physique came from New Zealand ; his game developed in England, where he graduated at Cambridge University. His was the sturdiest defence to a volleying assault I have ever seen. Could he have volleyed more himself, like W. M. Johnston, he would have been irresistible throughout his epoch. Without the generalship of Brookes, Beals Wright, or Tilden, he beat McLoughlin at Wimbledon in 1913 by a superb display of robust and co-ordinated driving. Incidentally he exposed the limitations of McLoughlin's service and volleying art, forestalling R. N. Williams in that achievement.

There is said to be no poison without its antidote. Provided the sting of McLoughlin's service could be extracted, there was just a chance for his opponent. And in the case of Norman Brookes, as both H. L. Doherty and Tilden proved, the most disturbing reply to his volleying campaign was a shrewd and well-placed lob. There has been no last word in lawn tennis yet ; therein lies its compelling interest—the Roland has been awaiting the Oliver. The first volleyer of all, Spencer Gore, was defeated in his second year because his adversary conceived the notion of raising the ball over his head ; and in the American championship final of 1926 at Forest Hills, the volleying skill of Jean Borotra, which had defeated both Johnston and Vincent Richards, was curbed by the calculating tossing of René Lacoste.

The supremacy of America in the lawn tennis world, like that of England, proved to be transitory. Previous to the Great War no American had succeeded in winning the men's championship at Wimbledon, and if the Davis Cup had been won back in 1913 the margin of victory was perilously small, while the failure which had attended three excursions to Australasia confirmed the view that Americans were more formidable in their own country than abroad. In the fifty months of the Great War the closure of competitive sport in Europe was complete ; in America the interregnum was much briefer. When the Armistice was declared all nations, irrespective of side, reacted from the strain and concentration of arms ; they turned with relief to the peaceful exercise of sport. America enjoyed this reaction like other belligerents, but she had the advantage of the shorter break, and her champions, when they emerged, were found to be in a higher class than their contemporaries. This was a natural and inevitable development ; it was assisted by the more intensive organisation of the game in the United States, an organisation which stimulated and extended the game in colleges and schools and did not neglect the opportunity for expansion in public parks.

Apart from these general agencies, all working to vivify American sport, the competition between the East and the West, as between England and Ireland a generation earlier, provoked a public interest which spurred on the players, increasing alike their skill and their zeal. Without connecting poles the current cannot circulate. History has shown that countries have increased their lawn tennis standard and prestige when they provided not only one champion of high calibre but another of equal, or nearly equal, strength who could extract the best from his opponent.

This matter of *vis-à-vis* has been paramount. The annual matches between Willie Renshaw and H. F. Lawford brought fame to the old centre court at Wimbledon ; they advertised lawn tennis in the early stages as nothing else could. If in the next decade Wilfred Baddeley had not been able to cross swords with Joshua Pim, the slump in British lawn tennis after the Renshaws retired would have been disastrous. Similarly, the matches between R. N. Williams of the East and M. E. McLoughlin of the West gave a fillip to American lawn tennis of a value which can only now be estimated. Later came the sequence of brilliant battles between W. T. Tilden of the East and

W. M. Johnston of the West. These championship encounters, like those in Paris between the leading Frenchmen, focused interest throughout the whole country. But their interest was not confined to the day of the fight. The champions' prowess both at home and abroad was an educational factor of ever-deepening force. For six consecutive years Tilden was invincible in Davis Cup and championship matches—a unique record, and much more impressive because other countries, like America, had been expanding their personnel, and the quality of opposition brought against the American champion was of the strongest.

William T. Tilden brought to the lawn tennis court physical strength and mental equipment of no ordinary pattern. These qualities assisted his progress ; without them he could not have maintained his remarkable record. But although Tilden's personality was distinctive, he did not climb the ladder of fame without absorbing the cumulative lessons of succeeding ages. That is to say, his game was developed and perfected after a natural and orderly evolution. Tilden's rise was not meteoric ; he had to serve a stern apprenticeship ; he had to pass through the mill. He had also, before his victorious career began, to reassert the orthodoxy of the all-court game. He had to restore " Larnedism " [W. A. Larned was champion of America for seven years] to American lawn tennis. He had to prove that solid and lasting success can only be constructed on a foundation of sound driving strokes.

The storming volleyer, novel and daring in his methods, had his triumphs both in America and in Europe, but his reign was threatened and could be interrupted by accurate ground strokes confidently and coolly controlled. The dynamic service of Gobert, covered by volleys of wonderful variety and finish, was challenged and ultimately frustrated by Wilding's piercing drives. McLoughlin found his match in Larned and then in Williams. Brookes was beaten by H. L. Doherty at Wimbledon and by Tilden at Auckland, and Borotra found in Lacoste the most disturbing party to his game.

Tilden drank deeply at the fountain of experience. A scientific student of the game, not only did he rely on his own contemporaries for the advancement of his own game, but, unconsciously, the virtues of former champions were transmitted to him through the medium of his older adversaries. But even Tilden, great player as he was, probably the greatest of his epoch, did not necessarily typify the highest potential art of the game. The future was seen to have something greater still in store. Tilden's stature assisted his service ; his long stride, apparently fortified against fatigue, was trained to produce the fiercest drives. But even a Goliath could have his limitations ; the sling of a lighter and more acrobatic David could be deadly.

§ 2

We have seen that no one nation could hold indefinitely the crown of lawn tennis. The emblem of power in half a century had already crossed the seven seas and returned. The very catholicity of the game, its extension in hidden places, its relation to psychological factors beyond the control of organisers, however zealous, made the champion breed uncertain ; and, of course, political and industrial unrest could affect the destiny of any sport.

The future of France on the lawn tennis court brightened appreciably in the decade following the War ; she had champions of youth, genius, and ambition. But the rise of France to the highest peak was no sudden, unsuspected movement. Her triumphs were preceded by many disappointments, even by an almost fatalistic feeling that her countrymen could never achieve signal success abroad. When the French first came to Wimbledon they used to cast wry faces at a slippery, oily surface upon which neither their feet nor their strokes would go right. Then the leading Frenchmen began to realise that a turf court was the championship court *par excellence* ; it responded to their delicacy of touch, extracted the refinements of their game, ministered to their buoyant nature.

It was almost the same thing when the French first went to America. They were disturbed by the American ball, disconcerted by the speed and " devil " of the American attack. But their enthusiasm and resource were such that they came again each year with strengthened hopes and sharpened weapons. If Mlle Lenglen could hold undisputed sway in the women's realm—and her career was a great incentive to her male contemporaries—they did not see why Frenchmen should not triumph as well. The first all-French final at Wimbledon was almost certain to bring another ; actually it had four successors in the next five years. An all-French final in New York was also seen.

It is not at all surprising that the French should play

lawn tennis well. The game lends itself directly to their mood for motion, their gift for swift repartee, their democratic bent. But before the War it was this vivacity which seemed to check their progress, robbing them of the highest honours. Perhaps the War chastened them ; at any rate it deepened their power of concentration and removed some of the insularity which handicapped their progress.

Yet we must go farther back than the War to trace the evolution of lawn tennis in France. The royal and ancient game of tennis—court tennis, that is—may have had its original root in Persia ; it was pursued in France centuries ago. A prototype of tennis, handball — or *longue paume*, as it was called in the Middle Ages—was played in France in the parks and fosses of the châteaux, indeed in any uncovered arena that could be found suitable for the purpose. Did not Louis X. die from a chill caught while playing in the forest of Vincennes in 1316? Was not Charles IX., when not campaigning or in action, always playing *la paume*, of which he was a devotee? *Longue paume* may have faded since there was last an enclosure for it in the Luxembourg Gardens ; the appeal of its principles remains ; its application to the French character is as insistent as ever. Long before Jean Borotra became famous the Basque provinces produced pelota players, whose quickness of foot and hand and surety of aim with the *schiesta* were the envy of Europe.

Philologists have, indeed, associated France with the origin of the word " tennis." It is now generally accepted that it is the French " *Tenez!* " (hold, take it) which the player of the fourteenth-century game is supposed to have called before serving. This etymology dates from Minsheu (1617) : " Tenez, *i.e.* hould, which word the Frenchmen, the onely tennis players, use to speake when they strike the ball at tennis." Professor Ernest Weekley declares [*Observer*, June 30, 1929] :

" The fact that Minsheu is our only authority for the French word in this special sense is not a serious objection. There is, in fact, plenty of indirect confirmation of his statement. It is known that tennis was introduced into Florence by French knights, *c.* 1325, and there called 'tenes.' In the *Colloquies* of Erasmus and in other early Latin mentions of the game we are told that the servers opened with the cry 'accipe' or 'excipe.' It is a reasonable inference that these Latin imperatives stand for French ' tenez.' The earliest English record is in Gower (*c.* 1400), who spells it ' tenetz,' the Anglo-French form of ' tenez ' (cf. our assets, from ' assez ').

" Spectators of a game played in a foreign tongue are apt to fasten on any oft-repeated word as the essential. There is the historical parallel of the Oriental gentleman who, after much watching of billiards, is still uncertain whether the game is called ' damn it ! ' or ' hard lines.' "

Professor Weekley also gives us the rational derivation of racket (Fr. *racquette*). It comes *via* Italian or Spanish from Arabic *rahat*, palm of the hand. *La Paume*, indeed, became so specialised in France as an aristocratic diversion that the office of professional or court-keeper was handed down from father to son ; hence the description " enfant de la balle " for one brought up from childhood to follow the family calling.

Tennis, indeed, has made many contributions to metaphor. We now bandy words, but our medieval ancestors " bandied " tennis balls. In the corresponding French " se renvoyer la balle," the origin is still on the surface. " Driven from pillar to post " comes from tennis. The original order was " from post to pillar " ; then the ball was " tost from pillar to post." The word " volley," suggesting in modern times musketry or expletive language, has an ancient tennis sense. Mashe wrote, in 1590, of " one that stands, as it were, at the line in a tennis court and takes everie ball at the volly."

There are no tennis lawns in France ; the game has been pursued on immutable wood or on *terre battue*. Therefore it is called tennis in France, although out of chivalry to English-speaking creators the federated governing body, which has its headquarters in Paris, is called the International Lawn Tennis Federation.

§ 3

Like Minerva from the head of Jove, lawn tennis is thought by many of its disciples to have sprung into active life about the date of the first Wimbledon meeting. The legend is only useful to emphasise the obscure origin of the pastime which obviously drew its roots, as it borrowed its implements, from much older games.

The lawn tennis racket and the net are primarily derived

from tennis. That game was originally played with the hand, gloved or ungloved. About the fifteenth century its devotees stretched thongs or strings of gut across their fingers. Then in the sixteenth century an Italian form of tennis was played with a *scanno*, a triangular contraption made of small wooden rods laid parallel and edgeways, up and down, but not across the frame. A modification of this invention is reported to have been forbidden in France, since it destroyed the balls and several rascals made money in bets by " killing " the ball literally.

From 1600 onwards there are many representations of early rackets. The first pictures show a straight-headed racket with a very short handle. A little later came the lop-sided shape, borrowed from tennis and associated with the early games of lawn tennis and used by its champions. The pear-shaped design, for tennis, is variously explained. Probably it came in with the cut stroke ; the player could always have the ball above his wrist. As lawn tennis gradually developed its own styles and strokes, shedding those associated with tennis and rackets [the original scoring of the game was that of rackets, with 15 aces up, but with the option of " setting " 3 or 5 at 13 or 14 all.], so it demanded a racket distinctive in shape, structure, and stringing. In 1874 the game was played, as a collection of rackets at Queen's Club, West Kensington, testifies, with a cross between a rackets racket and a tennis bat ; half a century has converted that weapon into an anachronism. Mr. Tilden's modern racket had a handle 4⅞ inches in diameter at its holding end and an " open throat " (*i.e.* a hollow V-shaped slot) to lessen the resistance of the atmosphere. Its weight was 13¼ ounces ; that of Mr. H. F. Lawford, the champion of 1887, was nearly 2 ounces heavier. The stringing of Mr. Tilden's racket, of Armour gut, was as tight as a drum. The stringing of Mr. Norman Brookes's racket, inclining to the oval in shape, was so loose that some of the Australian's strokes, made with a jerk and very little swing, bore an optical resemblance to the Lacrosse throw. M. Lacoste may employ a new racket for every set and profit by it ; some of the best lawn tennis has, nevertheless, been played with comparatively old and, in the American sense, loose rackets.

The idea of the net was also developed at tennis. A cord was first used, then a cord with a fringe on it. Its height was originally fixed by one player standing at the end of the court and being able to see just the end of the floor at the other and no more. Major Wingfield's net for lawn tennis, as shown in his specification for patent rights [the specification deposited by Major Walter Wingfield, M.V.O., is dated February 23, 1874, but the patent was not sustained], was 4 feet 8 inches high. It was oblong in shape and supported by two standards twenty-one feet apart. Triangular nets forming side walls to the court were placed at right angles to the oblong net on both sides—a device, cumbersome to erect, which did not survive the experimental stage.

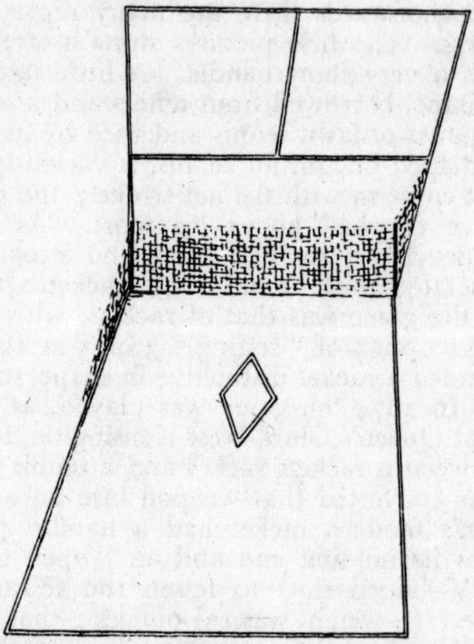

Fig. 4. MAJOR WINGFIELD'S COURT, 1874.

In 1875, when the M.C.C. Tennis Sub-Committee had drawn up rules of a game then without them, the length of the net was defined as 24 feet, its height at the posts as 5 feet, and its height at the centre as 4 feet. At the first championship meeting in 1877 the net was lowered in the centre to 3 feet 3 inches; a year later it lost 3 inches at the posts and 3 inches in the centre. In 1882, after joint communion between the M.C.C. and the All-England Lawn Tennis Club, there was a reduction at the posts to 3 feet 6 inches. An immediate effect of the change was seen in the Irish doubles championship at Dublin, when the brothers Renshaw, both camping on the service line, lost their titles ; their back-court opponents found loopholes down the side-lines. From 1882 onwards the net's height both at the posts and at the centre has remained inviolate.

The production of a game, not less than the evolution of a species, involves changes of more or less magnitude and a stream of tendency more or less continuous. But the significant fact may be recorded that, so far as lawn tennis is concerned, the main principles laid down by those who framed the rules for the first championship meeting have stood the test of time and are still law. Then the court was rectangular, measuring 78 feet long [Major Wingfield's court, hour-glass in shape, was 60 feet long and 30 feet at the baselines] and 27 feet wide ; the scoring of tennis was in vogue, and one fault was allowed to the server without penalty.

Time and experience have brought changes in other directions. The service line, 26 feet at the first championship meeting, was brought in to a distance of 21 feet in 1880 ; the limits of variation in the size and weight of the ball were amended at the same time, while, much later, a scientific test for regulating the bound of the ball was imposed.

The server's position has also undergone a radical change. In Major Wingfield's diagrammatic court he stood within a lozenge-shaped " service crease," placed between the net and the baseline. At the earliest Wimbledon the feet were straddled across the baseline, the ball, of course, in those days being delivered underhand, or occasionally, when enterprise was more rampant, with a sort of round-arm sweep. Three years later, when the overhead service was introduced, the " forward " foot was brought back to actual contact with the baseline. Subsequently both feet were required, under penalty, to be clear of the line while the advent of the storming volleyer brought specified restrictions of the feet's movements [see the *Rules of Lawn Tennis*, chapter 16]—restrictions which, while necessary, lend themselves, even in championship matches, to technical infringements of the law.

The rules also underwent amendment in respect to the service touching the net in delivery, to a player or his racket touching the net, to the ball passing round the net in play, to the permanent fixtures of the court, and in other minor directions. The cover of the ball is now stitchless ; until 1927, at any rate as far as Great Britain was concerned, the majority of covers were stitched and their flight and surface bound influenced accordingly. Such developments were more or less inevitable in a progressive age. The cardinal fact remains—and it is a tribute to the sagacious instinct of the original law-makers—that no fundamental change has been introduced, either in Britain or abroad, into the plan and apparatus of the court.

§ 4

We speak conventionally of lawn tennis being a British-born game. Its birthplace as a corporate and independent pastime undoubtedly belongs to Britain. But its roots go much deeper than, its conception was far antecedent to, the inventive acumen of Major Wingfield, the would-be patentee of Sphairistike in 1874. Major Wingfield deserves the credit of mankind for having designed a court and adapted an equipment—portable in its original form —by which a crude and barely recognisable imitation of the royal and ancient game of tennis was made possible on an open space without walls or cover. He was at best drawing on his own experience of the rackets and tennis courts. At the time neither he nor his friends, who experimented with and approved the new diversion, could have imagined that they were the Edisons of the athletic world. Because this is so, because its germs are traceable through the ages from the elementary ball game played by Nausicaa on the shores of Phæacia to the congeries of games, now organised, of which the principle has been the striking of and returning of a ball over a field or across a barrier, we can appreciate more clearly the reason for the wide and diffuse propagation of lawn tennis.

Regarded in this light and at a time when, through the agency of easier communication and travel, the nationals of all countries are disposed to link up and parade their hobbies as well as their habits, the development of lawn tennis loses much of its mystery. We know that, in a more dignified and difficult form, it was a " craze " in Europe four hundred years ago. The qualifications for a degree at the University of Paris were thus described by Rabelais :

> " So you have in your hand a racket,
> And a tennis ball in your pocket,
> And that you have skill to trip it
> In a low dance ; you will be allowed
> The grant of a licentiate's hood."

As in medieval Paris, so in more modern times. The disposition of governments, as of examiners, has been to encourage the games of democracy, and those who have shone at them have been favoured. Thus in lands where athletic culture has followed progressive tendencies in other directions, authority has conspired to give lawn tennis scope and popularity. The leading players of both sexes have been encouraged to test and mature their skill in the outer world ; and in the Davis Cup they found a friendly and ready-made forum for international rivalry. But in embracing the new pastime, often with fervour, these distant countries were not consciously following the example of an alien race. Rather were they expressing a cult, based on movement and competition, the practice of which was latent in their blood and history.

Just as some form of outdoor tennis seems to have been played from time immemorial, and on the mainland before it was played on the island, so we may assert with some confidence that the qualities, both physical and mental, requisite for championship skill, are not the prerogative of any one race. Having no local fount, the game could have no limited output.

CHAPTER
THREE

WOMEN AND A WORLD GAME

CHAPTER THREE

WOMEN AND A WORLD GAME

PROPHETS have told us that the hand that rocks the cradle will soon rule the world. The cynic might add that in that case we shall be governed by women lawn tennis players, for of all popular pastimes none has spread with such insidious strength. The innoculation is not confined to any one country, nor indeed to any one continent. In England and America the germ is paramount. There is no girls' school the inmates of which do not pursue the game, no college which does not boast its team. The Lenglen of England may not yet have been revealed, yet the raw material for champions is plentiful. But schools are not the only seed plot. The shop and the factory, the urban centres and the countryside, are paying every year a wider homage to lawn tennis.

The reasons are several, and some of them are complex. After the Great War there was a period of unrest, lasting for more than half a decade. The reaction from concentrated endeavour was fierce and prolonged. It was expressed in dancing, in cocktail drinking, and in other forms of irresponsible gaiety—perhaps inevitable, certainly stultifying. Then the wave of dissipation began to recede ; a more serious, a more thoughtful note permeated the land ; there was a demand for healthier recreations, for a normal antidote to the stress and strain of a busy life. Thus employers, no less than employed, encouraged the supply of recreative facilities. Every manufacturer and large store-keeper in England became, in theory if not in practice, a Henry Ford. He sought to lubricate the machinery of a workaday world with the oil of organised and subsidised pleasure. The municipalities, city, and village governments adopted the same line. They started to lay down hard courts for spring and autumn play, in many cases realising the capital expenditure by a moderate fee. The new zeal for lawn tennis thus created was reflected

D

in enlarged galleries at women's matches. The size of the crowd at the Wightman Cup contests, held on the famous centre court at Wimbledon, astonished even the executive ; it was more than four times as great as the crowd assembled for the same event two years earlier.

Another influence visible in both hemispheres was the steady propaganda of the popular Press. Lawn tennis was derided as an unmanly and unmannerly diversion. Rugby footballers were satirical at its expense ; they regarded it as effeminate, almost as a sign of degeneracy. Conservative headmasters of Public Schools retained this prejudice. They would not permit a square foot of their cricket fields to be used for its pursuit ; to them a lawn tennis racket was anathema. But the ranks of these bigots began to thin.

For as lawn tennis boys grew up they became lawn tennis fathers ; they felt disinclined to pay fees to institutions which did not encourage the pastimes of their own youth. The newspapers sensed the change ; not all of their proprietors were old men, born in the time when there was no lawn tennis. Besides, when a game had a family and communal interest, when the personalities of its champions were a theme for breakfast-table talk, when the face of Helen Wills became even better known in England than that of a cricket hero like Jack Hobbs, no editor worth his salt could afford to neglect the popular mind. Cricket remained the national summer game in England ; the rules of cricket were still synonymous to a code of honour ; but the public who watched it, and who compared it with a thrilling doubles match at Wimbledon between the leading Frenchmen and the leading Americans —it did not so much matter that these players were born across the seas—became a little restless, a little less contented, with the spectacle.

Nothing can be static and draw the breath of life. At present all that there is in lawn tennis—its movement, its international development, its medium for racial intercourse, its influence for peace and goodwill—has not been wholly revealed ; and when matter or mind is coming to maturity, its generating force, its capacity for strength, is at maximum. Lawn tennis may ebb and flow, but it is not likely to wane like dancing. The physical benefits which it confers are too obvious and too vibrant ; it is a daylight game, a game for sunshine, above all a game that promotes travel, knowledge and friendship.

There are shadows, of course, to every picture. A life devoted exclusively to lawn tennis may be the objective of some girls, whether American or British, Latin or Anglo-Saxon. The student of human nature can appreciate the lure ; the footlights and the films offer it in a similar degree. When young people, by the exercise of a physical art in public, can attract laudatory appreciation and become the theme for flattering paragraphs ; when their pictures are published broadcast, and their portraits thrown upon the screen ; when they are " boosted " at home and abroad—the fascination of the courts, the appeal to feminine vanity, is intelligible. This phase may be checked, it cannot be eliminated, by the legislative action of governing bodies. The forces of a lively world are too strong, the claim for freedom too insistent. But the moralist may utter his warning and perhaps suggest where organising enterprise may go too far.

Both in England and France, and now in other European countries, junior tournaments and junior competitions have been overdone. By this reflection I do not mean that boys and girls should not be allowed, like their elders, to match their skill and their ardour in friendly competitions for which a prize is bestowed on the winner. But these contests have been allowed to expand and multiply ; their local importance has been inflated, so that the winners of them have become heroes and heroines before their time. The fruit in many cases has been unripe ; it has been plucked too soon. The danger to character was exposed. The limelight has been altogether too bright for young eyes. Nor do these juvenile conquerors in a limited sphere, except in rare instances, develop into champions. More often than not they have won by the exercise of one stroke, or because they have been taller or broader than their fellows and have used a longer reach. Not enough discrimination has been shown over the entries or the ages at some of these junior tournaments ; nor have there been enough efficient umpires to go round, with the result that laws have been unconsciously broken, and bad habits ingrained. On the other hand let me be fair and say that many boys and girls, by assisting the management, have learnt and acquired executive duties under pleasant conditions ; their enthusiasm for the game has been kindled. If all cannot become champions of the playing art, they have become champions of its physical and mental culture.

Will women's lawn tennis reach a higher standard than

is current to-day? My own impression is that it must and will. I base this conclusion on various considerations. The first is that the leading players of to-day are physically stronger than the leading players twenty-five years ago. It is true that a champion of the latter era, Mrs. G. W. Hillyard, was a sprinter so agile that, taking a start of ten yards from any male competitor at an open tournament, she could beat him in a hundred-yard race. It is also true that Mrs. Hillyard, in her young days, could clear a five-foot gate with ease.

But this lady—a horsewoman of rare courage, by the way—was exceptionally versatile. Even so her service and driving strokes were much slower than those to be seen at present in a championship match, nor did she volley at the net. There were women volleyers in the past, and some of them—notably Miss Lottie Dod, the youngest champion ever crowned at Wimbledon, and Mrs. Larcombe—must have shone in the present ; for they had instinctive ability.

Yet, in the interval, the game on the women's side has moved forward to a higher plane. Dress reform, liberating limbs, has impelled new strokes, a quicker execution, a faster pace in every match. The evolution of men's play has influenced that of women. Señorita de Alvarez, the most brilliant stroke player of modern times, takes many balls on the rise ; she is a mistress of the half-volley achieved from a losing position on the court. If Miss Wills or Señorita de Alvarez, equipped as they were for the final at the new Wimbledon of recent years, were to be transferred to the old Wimbledon of two decades back, and were there to oppose players who were then in command, there is no doubt whatever that the " moderns " would gain a sweeping victory. The " ancients," however, might reply with justice, " If we had enjoyed the same freedom of dress, the same international practice, and the same stimulating influence, we might have held our own."

That hypothesis cannot be put to the test. Only this may be said—that the women players of yesterday were more accurate in their play, perhaps more intelligent, no less enthusiastic, than the players of to-day.

Of course there were fewer champions in the making ; the forcing frames were not so large, nor the sun, shining through the glass, as widely distributed. There was no thought of a French champion like Mlle Lenglen a quarter of a century ago. The child was not then trained with such meticulous care, nor did parents, looking forward, cast an eye on distant and ambitious goals. Mlle Suzanne Lenglen's influence on the game was broad and catholic. In history it will be regarded as epoch-making. For though the child of Compiégne did not love lawn tennis as intensely as her contemporaries—did not mind abandoning its pursuit before she was thirty years of age—she was the unconscious leader of a crusade. By her prowess and by her unbeaten record at Wimbledon for six years, by the legends associated with her career and by the theatrical atmosphere generated round her matches, she advertised women's lawn tennis in a way and to an extent that no other agency could have achieved.

For those six years—in Europe, at any rate—Mlle Lenglen *was* lawn tennis. She blazed a trail throughout the world —that is, in every country to which the tale of her triumphs was carried. When she embraced professionalism she shed much of her magic power. It takes two to make a quarrel, and two of the same calibre to make a first-class lawn tennis match. Isolated as Mlle Lenglen became through her own action, she could only perform, in America and elsewhere, as an exhibitor of facile stroke-play. The lust and lure of battle was removed, and both Mlle Lenglen and the spectators—much fewer in numbers than at Wimbledon and St. Cloud—were conscious of the change.

Yet the example of Mlle Lenglen remained. She bred a host of imitators—girls eager to emulate her success and to acquire her spoils, but girls who had not undergone the same disciplinary training which M. Charles Lenglen imposed. His daughter has often been described as a genius. In the qualified sense, if genius is the art of taking pains, that description is true. But she was in actuality a "made" player, just as René Lacoste was a "made" player. Both these French ornaments of the game were delicate in youth ; both gained strength and agility by careful and systematic training. Of Helen Wills, now Mrs. Moody, the same may be said, except that Miss Wills, like Anthony Wilding, was a strong child, allowed to develop on her own lines.

There have been very few outstanding geniuses in women's lawn tennis. You could almost count them on the fingers of one hand. Miss Lottie Dod was one and the earliest ; she reigned at a period when international competition was virtually unknown. I think Miss May Sutton, afterwards Mrs. Bundy, was another ; for although she did not possess all the modern strokes, she did not need the aid of any coach—she had tennis inside her. The same may be said of Mrs. Lambert Chambers, who won the championship seven times at Wimbledon. She was essentially a backcourt player, but she had the tennis brain highly developed. Señorita de Alvarez is unquestionably a genius. She required little practice to exploit her versatile art. Miss Esther Heine, of South Africa, was born a player.

No doubt there are many young champions now in the making; they await only an essential challenge in the best company. In America, in Europe, in Australia, in South Africa, and possibly in the Orient, are girls who, given the opportunity, will blossom into players of real eminence. The firmament of so-called stars may then become so enlarged that the lustre of present stars may be dimmed. New lights may shine in new places.

CHAPTER
FOUR

STYLE AND THE RACKET HOLD

CHAPTER FOUR

STYLE AND THE RACKET HOLD

IT is a moot question to what extent a game may be taught by the written word. The majority of champions are born and not made—by which is meant that if physical tendencies provoking skill are not traceably inherited, the will-power needed to acquire skill through industry and patience springs from native character. Since Nature is stronger than mankind and natural evolution may be delayed by artificial stimulant, one is reluctant to dogmatise where the science of bodily exercises is concerned. And in regard to a pastime so cosmopolitan in its pursuit as lawn tennis—a game, moreover, that has steadily extended its scope for rapid and synthetic movement—it might be unwarrantable to claim for any one style of play that it represents the summit of human endeavour.

Physiologists credit us with at least seven senses, four of which enter largely into bat and ball pastimes, and their satisfaction is the chief source of the pleasure of play. These are sight, touch, the sense of balance, and the muscular sense. "They work together," says A. E. Crawley, "now more, now less; the reflective centres of the brain do not intervene except to formulate plans of action, changes of play, and general policy. Everything else is done mechanically, instinctively, unconsciously, by the muscles, in silent and perfect obedience to the locomotor centres, the nerve-systems which work the muscles. The eye is the 'finder,' the focus of operations is the ball to be hit, or the mark to be attained. The mechanical delicacy of the whole process is shown by the concentration involved, and by the fact that the least bit of grit will throw it out of gear" [*The Book of the Ball* (Methuen)].

When the centipede began to count its steps and reckon their alternations, it discovered that it could not walk at all. "We fail," said James, the psychologist, "whenever we are preoccupied with the way in which the movement will feel. We pitch or catch the better, the more exclusively optical our consciousness is. Keep your eye on the place aimed at and your hand will fetch it ; think of your hand and you will miss." The instructor who overloads the pupil's mind with either the spoken word or written word may prevent or delay progress on natural, self-prompted lines.

But when a game has reached maturity, when the wild oats of its experimental youth have been sown, so to speak, the fact implies a certain stability of style and a certain standardisation of stroke. The laws of lawn tennis have not been altered fundamentally since they were first drawn up, neither have the basic principles of the game. Dynamic forces do not change with succeeding epochs ; motion and matter are still in conflict, yielding the same results. The interchange of racket blows on the ball still means the compression and restitution of its shape. According to the direction of those blows and the force generated, so does the ball respond in action. According to the character of the blow and the floor on which it falls, the ball may slide, roll, or spin. The science of spin or rotation, while better understood to-day by more players, is as old as the oldest sphere, the earth itself ; nor was it unexplored by the earliest champions.

Admitting these static laws of Nature the searcher after correct " form " will not go far wrong—may, indeed, see the light—if he examines the methods of great players, always bearing in mind that they, like himself, have served an apprenticeship in the field of experience. An inherited aptitude for ball-games may permit a man to pass his " Little Go " without cramming ; only application harnessed to his talent will permit him to graduate ; only more application, both of mind and body, will win him an honours degree.

If a child of tender years is offered the handle of a racket, its possessive instinct will probably guide the palm to somewhere near its middle—there is felt to be less likelihood of escape in this position. Even people of riper age, who have never swung a racket before, will, unless they are unconsciously imitating a player, grasp the handle well above its leather-covered end. When example or a friendly voice comes to their aid and the grip is lowered to the extremity of the handle, the first tendency will be to drop the head towards the ground and to think of the racket performing the same function as a croquet mallet or a hockey stick. On the approach of the ball the raw recruit, facing the firing-line for the first time, will probably consider that its point of contact with the court is his primary objective. Consequently, he will almost certainly advance to meet it facing the net, and will be discomforted to find that Will o' the Wisp was not a more elusive quarry.

Women beginners (not young girls, for they would seem to be more impressionable and, therefore, more observant) are especially prone to start their lawn tennis career with a vertical or drooping racket, moving pendulum-fashion, and only calculated to make contact with the ball when its flight crosses miraculously the path of their semi-circular swing. In many cases tender wrists reject subconsciously the horizontal swing, but the original vertical swing among women (and even among some men) was possibly due to the fact that most of the early women players (and some of the early male players) exchanged a mallet for a racket. Young women of later generations had no such handicap ; they acquired the orthodox style much more rapidly and with much less travail. They had, indeed, unlike the majority of boys, received initiation at school.

The Orthodox Style.

What is orthodox style and what are its advantages? Orthodoxy means an accepted faith, a doctrine which time and experience have vindicated. Lawn tennis is a relatively young game, but it has lived long enough to indoctrinate definite themes of play. Its pursuit is based on principles firm and foolproof enough to be understood by intelligent persons, and the fact that successive types of champions reveal a common adherence to those principles and are inspired by their practice is an adequate tribute to their value.

Different nationals, like different groups within the same nation, may adopt distinctive styles of play ; they tend to eradicate those differences as and when they come into frequent contact with styles which expose the deficiencies of their own style. Youth, of course, is more malleable in this respect, but youth is not always most observant nor has it the disciplined will which age encourages. Players beyond the first blush of youth have often remodelled their style, shedding some awkward or laboured stroke, or acquiring some new weapon of attack or defence, by grasping the principles which underlie orthodox stroke production. These principles may be treated under three headings :

(a) Hold of the Racket.
(b) Footwork.
(c) Meeting and Striking the Ball.

Physically speaking there is only one grip of the racket. All grips, expressing the capacity of the hand, depend mainly on the " opposed position " of the thumb in relation to the fingers.

The Grip of the Racket.

A preliminary notion of the racket grip may be obtained by grasping a hammer, a sabre, or an axe, and by jerking such an instrument up and down while the handle is gripped between the forefinger and the thumb. When these are half open and parallel to one another they form three sides of a long or flat rectangle—a rectangle that just fits the handle. If we regard the handle as a rectangle, one short side fits the space between the base of the thumb and the base of the forefinger ; the long sides rest along the second phalange of the thumb and the third phalanges of the fingers, respectively. " It is as if you were holding a sabre with the grip appropriate to a cut, and were then to hit the object with the flat instead of with the edge " [*The Complete Lawn Tennis Player*]. The hand, with the thumb and all the fingers, is turned slightly forward ; the forefinger, acting as a strut or prop, is a little farther up the handle than the thumb. An even rougher method of fitting is to place the hand on the handle in such a position that the line which runs between the thumb and forefinger to the centre of the wrist (the line of life) lies along the junction of the ash and mahogany. The heel of the hand, but not the little finger, which will be about an inch higher, rests on the leather.

Backhand Grip.

In outline this is the orthodox method of hold for the primary, or forehand drive. That for the backhand drive is the same, but reversed. That is, with the racket remaining at rest in the same position, the hand is turned backward (counter-clockwise) on the handle for a quarter-circle. The thumb shifts to the back of the handle in the position corresponding to that of the forefinger in the forehand grip ; acting as a strut or prop, its extreme point is only a little higher up the handle than the encircling forefinger.

The ball of the thumb will be almost entirely on the long side, the first phalanges of the fingers gripping the short side of the handle. Fitting by lines, the line of life will be along the junction of the ash and mahogany opposite to that indicated for the forehand grip.

It is not essential to have the thumb up the handle. "Thumb-up" players, of whom there are several in the front rank, find an extra security for service, smash, and backhand volley, as well as for the backhand drive; but W. T. Tilden, who had a fine backhand drive, did not advance the thumb, and it may be suggested that by not doing so he ensured less rigidity of hold and facilitated the automatic, almost unconscious turn-over for the production of the forehand drive.

Fixed or Movable Backhand Grips.

As to the relative merits of fixed and movable "grips," expert opinion favours the latter, although championships have been won by players addicted to the former. Of acknowledged masters through succeeding epochs the Renshaws, the Dohertys, W. T. Tilden, R. Lacoste, H. Cochet, and Mlle Lenglen all shifted their holds, in greater or less degree, to achieve "double-winged" strokes. Even W. M. Johnston, using the grip common on the Pacific Coast of America, which does not reverse the racket face for the forehand and backhand shots, was not "uncompromisingly Western."

The views of champions, past and present, on this subject may be quoted:

H. W. W. Wilberforce (Doubles Champion at Wimbledon, 1887).—"I am firmly persuaded that with an unchanged grip there is less power of hitting, and, moreover, the racket is prevented from meeting the ball full, that is to say, without causing a twist. To put twist on a stroke is to sacrifice power without obtaining any corresponding advantage, those strokes only excepted where it is desired that the ball shall drop close to the net."

R. F. Doherty.—"There is no doubt it is better to change the grip a little. We might say, however, that at the beginning the less change the better, so that the learner may not have too many things to attend to. The Baddeleys never changed their grip at all, and it seems to have been partly owing to this that their backhand strokes were their weakest."

W. T. Tilden.—" My belief is that all great players vary their grips often, according to the shot they are playing and the spin they intend to put on the ball. I know that while the foundation of my game is based on the Eastern [*i.e.* East of America] grip, I often use a Western grip to obtain a certain spin on a forehand drive, while for certain sliding shots I will use an English grip. Every player should have a certain definite foundation for his style and then develop along the lines that best suit his physical and mental equipment. I am a great believer in individualism in tennis, so long as it has the sound foundation of form behind it. Work out your own racket grips along your personal views, just as long as you have a safe, sane theory to fall back upon in time of stress " [*Match Play and the Spin of the Ball* (American Lawn Tennis)].

R. Lacoste.—" Choose a grip for striking the ball on the forehand stroke and, by turning the handle of the racket in the hand to the extent of about a quarter of a turn, a grip for playing the backhand stroke. Do not strike the ball on the forehand stroke and on the backhand stroke with the same side of the racket. Do not try to hold your racket in the same way for the execution of every stroke " [*Lacoste on Tennis* (Ed. J. Burrow)].

Mlle Lenglen.—" If for a backhand stroke you have retained the same grip as for the forehand stroke, the face of the racket will be inclining ; if it is not, then the wrist will feel cramped. . . . While bringing the racket round from the forehand—all the movements, remember, must be done simultaneously, not as bits by themselves, or you would be tied up in contortions—the grip must be changed, so that the ball of the thumb rests on the part of the octagon of the handle which is away from the direction of the stroke and on the top. Thus you have between the ball of the thumb and the first finger the three top sides of the octagon " [*Lawn Tennis : the Game of Nations* (Harrap)].

These views, voicing competent opinion over a period of forty years—the best part of the life of championship lawn tennis—teach the same lesson in different eras—that of changing the racket's hold in order that the principles of correct stroke play may be served. Later on we shall refer to the purposeful application of spin—top-spin and back-spin—and the relation of its production to the hold. Here we are only concerned with the creation of cardinal strokes—the forehand and backhand drive—the foundation of the game—a prime necessity for those who aspire to pursue it.

The beginner is not invited to imitate slavishly the grip of any one teacher or any one champion. The essence of good style is freedom, of ease of action without conscious effort. The great majority of champions have been self-taught; at any rate they have corrected faults and mastered technical problems by personal observation either on the court or off it. The objective for all advancing players must be increased steadiness and power and an extension of strokes which equips their owner for any and every emergency. If a study of orthodox methods is the surest road to the desired goal, then our faith in orthodoxy is vindicated; we may listen to the voice of history.

CHAPTER
FIVE

FOOTWORK AND STROKE PRODUCTION

CHAPTER FIVE

FOOTWORK AND STROKE PRODUCTION

THE feet are the pivot on which the body turns. Jointly or severally they constitute its axis ; like the peg of a spinning-top their balance is essential for the rotation of the body. But, unlike the top, they have supporting and correlated arms which form, with the body's trunk to which both are connected, a complex interacting mechanism.

Nominally lawn tennis is played with the hands, which grasp and control the weapon of attack ; actually, since the body, like the ball, is in movement most of the time, the legs and feet play a part no less important in the production of the stroke. What is perfect timing, the essence of good play, but an effective distribution of weight through the hips from one foot to another—the creation of speed through a balanced movement.

Good footwork means good armwork, for though it might be possible to make a respectable drive with both feet clamped down on the court, the game does not permit the static positions of croquet ; the feet must be free to move in pursuit of the ball to any section of the court—in theory they must be as fluent as the ball itself. Indeed, it is pedestrically rather than manually that the game has developed in recent years. Its athletic—one may almost say its acrobatic—qualities have been realised ; a quickening of every movement, virtually of every muscle, has resulted.

The earlier champions may have executed their strokes as skilfully and as delicately as the later ; behind those strokes was just as much power and resolution ; their mechanics have not changed. But wider and keener competition, more practice in the best company, improvement in equipment, superior physical training, and greater fervour expressed by larger crowds, have intensified and amplified stroke action. The service-cum-volleying cult in singles, introduced largely by the American players, while proving to be only transitory, had a permanent effect in increasing mobility. The server, who seemed to regard the orthodox ground stroke almost with reproach, rushed to the net with the impetus of a Rugby footballer —he would sometimes rush back nearly as fast in pursuit of a lob.

The development of the service itself also energised footwork; for a man who delivered the " googly," so fashionable in the first decade of the century, was required to balance and control his toes in a manner unknown to the older servers, while the " striker-out," meeting the missile at its exploding end, was required to spring much farther in its pursuit in order to gain contact. These pedalian gyrations to execute the initial stroke on both sides of the court—on the service and its return—naturally infused livelier footwork in every other stroke of the game. The spirit of attack engendered by the service remained; simultaneously the receiver attempted to turn or nullify the service attack by quicker movement; as the rallies were shortened by a rapid desertion of base—as the rate of mortality increased, so to speak—the physical effort to sustain them and avert disaster was extended.

Practice for the Novice.

Of course, the novice should not be asked to concern himself with these embroideries of the game. He must look at its plain and simple garb. It were better at first if he did not consider his feet at all; for if he begins to shift them ever so little before he can swing the racket intelligently to meet and return a moving ball purposely aimed in his direction, his progress may be arrested at the start. It is not essential for swing-learning to strike at a real ball or to go out on a real court. Even the racket (which is really an artificial extension of the arm) may be dispensed with by the absolute tyro. Fives is an ancestor of tennis; first, in the privacy of your own room, employ the hand to sweep the air. The motion should not be fast or wild; it should be slow and measured. The arm should be slightly crooked at the elbow, with the hand raised at right angles to the body, presenting a perfectly flat face to an imaginary ball. The left shoulder will be pointing to an imaginary net; the beginner, before he swings, will be facing the imaginary side-line. Thus standing (easily, but not troubling at the moment about his feet or their position) he may practise the rhythm and balance of the swing—the backward movement, which should not be too deep (about a quarter-circle) and the return movement, including the follow-through, which should be in the same orbit, completing a half-circle.

The skeleton movement for the backhand stroke may be practised and its principle grasped in the same way. The shoulder will still point to an imaginary net (that is, the direction in which the ball will be propelled) ; the exerciser, his body reversed, will still be facing an imaginary side-line ; the back of the hand, instead of the palm, will be used as the "striking" rod. But the arm, for the preliminary swing (the pressing back of the spring, as it were), will be bent across the body rather than stretched away from it, as in the forehand exercise, and the finger-tips, before they swing outward on the return journey, will be almost in a line with the left shoulder. Again the half-circle will be completed in one movement.

The Mechanics of the Tennis Stroke.

The would-be player must grasp the mechanics of the lawn tennis stroke ; the knowledge will help to cultivate a style that, when he advances to match play, will assist his rapid development and prevent the growth of unorthodox or laboured strokes, which increase materially the physical strain. The effortless ease with which champions make their strokes is the result, not of any super-human attribute, but of mechanical laws operating through a body that does not offer them a fettering resistance ; these champions are merely expressing a science applied to the natural resources of their own limbs.

The Classic French Style.

There is no question that the style and mechanics of the lawn tennis stroke are founded on the style and mechanics of the tennis stroke—a stroke which man has executed for centuries past. The French pursued tennis, as we have seen, in the dim past ; their natives have an instinctive penchant for playing the lawn tennis stroke ; and the fact that their champions have style at once graceful and unexhausting inclines the investigator to accept French players—those of the orthodox school, that is—as models, or, at any rate, as standards, for commendation. This is not to say that every French champion has every stroke known in the game, nor uses each with maximum speed and control ; exclusive genius is not the prerogative of any one country. But it does suggest that players like Mlle Lenglen, R. Lacoste, and H. Cochet, all of transcending ability, provide in their not dissimilar styles and methods guiding principles which the world at large may study and follow.

It will be found in examining the stroke production of the leading French players, as of their predecessors, the Doherty brothers in England, that balance, poise, and rhythm are its salient characteristics. The quality of sheer force, that is to say the " hit " as opposed to the " sweep," is absent from their accurate and finely-controlled strokes. The basis of the movement is swing, and the swing is in the nature of a pendulum movement on a horizontal plane. It produces, simultaneously and without conflict, both power and rhythm. If we can learn its basic secret we are on the right road to rational initiation.

Remembering what was written in a previous chapter, the reader may be invited to note that the original swing was made in a vertical line, like the movement of a clock's pendulum ; some of the first players in the pre-Doherty era never deserted this style. The stroke known as " The Irish Drive "—most effective on wet courts when the ball kept low—was a product of the vertical style. The ball was struck at its lowest point with a vertical swing, followed on contact with a pronounced upward lift of the racket. This movement compelled the player to strike the ball very close to his side. When volleying increased its range and power, the effort of resistance—rapid time forming the essence of the contract—caused the ball to be met earlier and at the top of its bound. The result was a marked, if gradual, change in the player's stance ; he stood (or advanced) nearer to the spot of the ball's bound and receded from its path at the side ; he made the stroke along a horizontal rather than along a vertical line.

The Saving of Effort.

The French school, as represented by Lacoste and Cochet, developed this method to a degree which makes the methods of their predecessors, if not obsolete, at least old-fashioned. Their racket is " swung through " the ball rather than " swung at " it. There is a smooth, even movement of the shoulders, initiated by a turn of the hips, which pivot on the legs. There is the forcing forward of the forearm and the racket to meet the ball. The racket, so to speak, is absorbed in the general mechanism of the whole body ; it is merely an adjunct of the arm rather than an independent weapon.

Such a process of stroke production, there is little doubt, ensures maximum of control, while, because of its neatness and fluency, conserving energy. The player's whole arm (forearm, elbow, and wrist) act as a kind of "shock-absorber" by which the impact of the ball, however severe, is resisted and controlled. At the same time the rotation of the hips and shoulders gives sufficient propulsion to the racket to make the ball's return very speedy. The pace on the ball, still rising, is considerable ; it may be used and absorbed in the return stroke, which will then gain in speed and surprise.

Power of Stroke.

The pendulum-like swing of the arm and racket is produced by three distinct but correlated movements, felt from the feet upwards into the shoulder and through the arm. These, which generate power, are :

(1) A slight turning movement of the right hip against the left knee and foot, towards the direction of the ball.

(2) A considerably longer movement back and away from the ball made by the left hip turning against the right knee and foot, by which the arm and racket are brought back for the stroke.

(3) The turning of the right hip against the braced left knee and foot, which causes the shoulder to swing round, and so brings round the arm and racket in the actual stroke.

The first movement is merely preparatory, and, as it were, starts the pendulum-like swing of the shoulders and hips (*e.g.* the left, right, and left of the golf drive).

The second generates the power for the stroke by creating tension in the right side of the body.

The third releases this tension, and so uses the power generated by the previous movement for the stroke.

This pendulum movement can only be made by the use of practically every part of the player's body.

Footwork.

One may add here that whenever the player has to move into another position to make his stroke, the action of running helps the necessary swinging movement of the shoulders, hips, and arm in making the stroke. All the player should then remember is to steady himself in his run upon the foot farther from the net, when his body is turned sideways to the line of the ball's course—*i.e.* upon the left foot for the backhand and upon the right foot for the forehand stroke. In this way he will find that he can gain the power to make the stroke on the farther foot and use it when he puts his weight upon the nearer foot in turning his hips and shoulders round, with his racket in the actual production of the stroke.

In order to obtain the necessary leverage for the stroke, the feet must hold on to the ground firmly, with the ankles flexible to allow power to be transmitted up the legs to the hips, by which the shoulders are turned, and with them the arm, elbow, and racket. The knees should be slightly bent throughout all the movements of the stroke ; the player's balance (as in skating) is thus secured on the hips, legs, and feet.

The lower part of the body from the hips should be regarded as the pedestal upon which the upper part above the waist can turn to make the strokes. The power to effect this turning movement of the hips and shoulders is derived from the knee muscles, which, for this purpose, should always be slightly bent. Moreover, in order to obtain this power, the knees should be used one against the other ; they should be alternately tensed and relaxed in the course of the three movements of the swing.

The knee muscles are enabled to play their part because of the grip of the feet upon the ground and because the ankle joints are kept as flexible as possible. By moving one knee in towards the other, which must remain braced firmly to meet it, the turning movement of the hips begins ; the hips in turn move the shoulders, which move the arms and racket.

Thus the power for the stroke is generated in reality by the feet, legs, and hips, and is passed up to the shoulder, elbow, and arm, which distribute it for the production of the stroke.

In this method the arm below the elbow and the racket are never allowed to free themselves forward of their own initiative ; they only move after the shoulder has begun the turning movement towards the ball. The stroke becomes more of a " sweeping through " movement than a sharp, crisp hit made by the hand and wrist.

At this point, when describing the method by which power for the stroke is gained, it is as well to mention that the player's weight must be transferred from the foot upon which he has made his back swing, either by a definite movement from one foot to the other, as in the backhand stroke, or by the "rippling" feeling of the power passed up to the shoulders in making the forehand stroke when played off the right leg. Nothing should ever be done above the waist until the pedestal, as represented by the left leg in the backhand, and either of the two legs and feet in the forehand shot, has received the weight of the player's body, and so is prepared to stand the strain of the turning movement of the hips and shoulders above them. Then, and then only, may the shoulder and upper arm bring round the forearm and racket to meet the ball. This is the old advice of the golf professional: "Hips through first. The arm and club will follow."

By this method the stroke becomes far more delicate, the player's "touch" is greatly increased, and the greatest possible control can be exercised over every shot. It explains why, with quick footwork and the rhythm thus given, the French school of players have become the most efficient, as well as the most graceful, in the world.

In some players of the Lenglen type the lower arm, wrist, and racket are treated like the lash of a whip, and follow the stock, which is represented by the shoulder and the upper arm in the circular movement of the swing. In other words they are not allowed to impart any of the force of a blow to the ball; they only obey, without any initiative of their own, like the lash of a whip, the movement of the shoulder, which obtains its power up from the feet by an extremely lissom body-action.

Grasping this principle of power transmission, the reader will not need to trouble a perplexed mind over elaborate footwork. He will indeed find his feet reconciling their positions more or less unconsciously to the strokes as they are prepared for and produced; and when he examines the action photographs reproduced in this volume—pictures taken for the most part during actual match-play—his mystification at the apparently abnormal posture of some of the feet may disappear. He will then realise that balance of a body in motion does not depend on its point of contact with the ground; equilibrium is maintained in and through the moving body. That is only another way of saying that quick footwork is absolutely essential; for slow and heavy footwork will retard the action of the machine above.

CHAPTER
S I X

FURTHER DRIVING PRINCIPLES

CHAPTER SIX

FURTHER DRIVING PRINCIPLES

IN order to execute the movements described in the last chapter to the best advantage—that is, with the best results—attention must be directed to various auxiliary points. Their consideration is essential if the complete success of the stroke is to be achieved.

Balance.

A factor of supreme importance is the player's balance throughout all the movements of the stroke. The two disturbing factors are stiffness and " lop-sidedness " ; the presence of either will be fatal to a smoothly-played and strainless stroke. The human organism was created on a system of duality—that is, on twofoldness in the unity of being. The influence of balance pervades the body and governs the senses. The player who overlooks this axiom and regards the " racket " side of his body as an independent mechanism, which can function without regard to the " non-racket " side, is tilting against the laws of Nature and must always invite physical strain.

Unless both arms and both legs take their proper share in the production of the stroke, just as both eyes are used to follow the flight of the ball and both ears signal its contact with the racket, an abnormal result will follow. The harvest of incomplete or " one-winged " players is due to the neglect of this fundamental principle in the early stages of learning ; and one may add that many coaches, not themselves conscious of its importance in instructing youth, are responsible for evolving many ungainly competitors at open tournaments.

But proper body balance is not wholly dependent on the movements of the legs and arms ; the trunk which connects them must, as in dancing, be pliant, turning, as we have seen, in sympathy with the general exercise. The best players—those with the easiest style and those who tire least—are conscious of playing the stroke with the whole body and not of using only a section of it. Incidentally, of course, it is this sense of completeness which adds to the pleasure of "style." It is also the reason why lawn tennis, if played in good style, can give physical exercise, and with it health, to the whole body. Fatigue, in other words, is induced by "lop-sidedness," by the over-exertion of one section and the comparative idleness of the other.

Position for Receiving.

This all-body "feeling" may be generated by the preparation of the player in making the stroke. Thus, before the ball comes to hand, he should cultivate the habit of lowering the hips—as in beginning the sitting down position. The knees should be slightly bent and the feet placed firmly on the ground, with the balance rather forward on the balls of the toes—never up on the toes at the start of the movement. This slightly crouching position permits an easy poise for the upper part of the body, aiding its balance and allowing the shoulders to be turned round by hip rotation when this complementary action is required.

Position of the Racket.

The arm with the racket attached should always be kept bent at the elbow in order that the shoulders may turn it freely. If the racket head be not held above the wrist—and many players hold it below the wrist—a certain drag or strain on the shoulder or elbow must result. One of the cumulative effects of this strain is "tennis elbow," to which some reference is made in a later chapter.

The hold of the racket, discussed in Chapter Four, has an important bearing on the production of those strokes of which the French players are masters and which are here put forward as models. Uniformity of grip is not to be expected and may not be desired, but a grip that assists the complete anatomical movement is obviously to be preferred. The handle should not be held in a manner which golfers call "the palm grip." It should lie easily, yet firmly, across the hand in a diagonal line, the thumb and middle finger acting as the gripping agents and the third and fourth fingers not grasping but controlling the handle. By crooking the forefinger the handle will rest in a kind of cradle ; it will be supported comfortably and without strain.

The method of the racket hold reveals its significance

when the subsequent path of the racket is considered. Unless its head is supported above the line of the wrist, the racket cannot be carried back in that circular action of the elbow and forearm which ensures the free action of the shoulder-blade and creates in the hips that motive power which enables the body to turn for the stroke. Balance and rhythm, which promote perfect timing, cannot be obtained *after* these preliminaries ; they come as their sequel. In other words, a good stroke is born before the ball is struck.

Path of the Racket.

In considering the actual path of the racket for the production of the stroke, one may use the simple design of a clock face. If the player's racket is facing twelve o'clock, with his feet pointing in that direction, he will move the racket round and back in a quarter-circle to three o'clock and then push it straight across the face to nine o'clock. This combined motion indicates, roughly, the circular preparatory movement of the back swing, and the forward action of the stroke itself. It may be practised with equal benefit on the backhand.

Action of the Shoulder Blade.

The importance of the shoulder blades has been mentioned. Although a seemingly obscure portion of the anatomy—and the average coach is inclined to think exclusively in terms of "arms and legs"—the shoulder blade's behaviour has a material effect on the player's balance and on the accuracy of his stroke. To French champions like Lacoste and Cochet it is virtually the key position. By consciously employing it they can adjust their distance away from the ball to a nicety, thus avoiding a loss of balance by a last-second stretch forward on to the toes, or, by straightening the elbow joint, forfeiting power in the swing.

If the ball's distance has been judged correctly—that is, to permit the hips to turn easily—the shoulder blade's controlling influence will be realised. It will prove to be the agent by which the racket is directed along the line of the ball's path at the moment of impact. The circular character of the swing will thus prevent the racket from being drawn across the ball's line, as it otherwise would if the shoulder blade had not promoted an extra adjusting "stretch" exactly when the racket meets the ball at the moment of the actual stroke.

The arm and racket, having been swung round by the pivoting of the body at the hips, is extended by this ability to stretch from the shoulder blade and the upper arm, thus allowing the racket to be pushed along the straight line of the ball's course and meeting it with a full, instead of with an indirect, blow. The circular swing of the racket, caused by hip and shoulder rotation, is thus interrupted only by the influence of the shoulder blade, which pushes the arm outward for the racket to meet the ball. The circular path of the racket is resumed in the "follow-through," arm and racket having been guided by the original turning movement of the shoulders.

Rhythm.

Rhythm is an essential factor in the lawn tennis stroke. We speak of a player's rhythmic strokes when we mean that he controls a measured or timed movement, a regulated recurring motion. To produce it sympathy and co-operation between the composite parts of the body are, as in the case of an orchestra, necessary. Disruption, like discord, is caused if the intervals between the successive and sequential movements in stroke production are not employed in the proper way.

If it be agreed that the pendulum swing is the basis of the lawn tennis stroke, every movement must be synthetic; the various elements must be united into a compound. After the first preparatory exercise has been executed, its successor must follow naturally and without effort; the whole notion must have no conscious break or pause. A simple analogy is that of a person walking. Here is Nature's rhythm unconsciously expressed. Think of the lawn tennis stroke in the same way, and the problem of its cultivation will be found to be much less difficult.

Walking, in its time and order, provides a "natural movement." One therefore suggests that the drive, as previously described, should be considered in sequential terms. The whole body is utilised. Power is generated in the feet and legs and is transmitted upwards to the arms and racket—the time and order have the simple sequence of walking. This was the unsophisticated secret of Mlle Lenglen's art, as it is of Lacoste's. The rhythm of their strokes originates in the feet, since the ground is the fulcrum for all leverage; it moves upwards through the hips and the shoulders to the arms and the racket; whether in fast or slow time the communication is orderly and co-operative.

Three-Movement Rhythm.

To acquire this rhythmic power the player, in the early stages, may employ counting terms. Thus, in the fore-hand stroke, when he makes the little preparatory turn to the left, slightly turning his right hip towards the ball, he may count *One*.

With the feeling of a swinging movement initiated in his feet and body, he then turns the left hip against the right knee, leg, and foot, at the same time bringing back his arm, racket, and shoulder in a circular arc. Here he will count *Two*.

By this time the feeling of swing in the shoulders will have so far increased that before he can comfortably make the shoulder, arm, and racket return for the forward swing, which is the stroke itself, he must make the smallest pause, with all the weight poised on the right foot and all the tension residing in the right knee and leg. The force generated by the previous movements, concentrated here, will, when transmitted upwards, cause the hip to come round and bring the shoulders and arm forward for the making of the actual stroke. During this little interval—when the arm and hand holding the racket are allowed to find whatever level is necessary for contact with the ball—the player counts *And*. When the turn is made which causes the shoulder and racket to come round for the stroke, he counts *Three*.

The Return of the Rising Ball.

This three-movement rhythm, it will be found, is the basic principle of sympathetic movement of arms, legs, and feet in virtually every branch of athletic exercise or sport. The modern method of striking the lawn tennis ball as it rises from the court is not hindered but assisted by its adoption. The time occupied over the preparatory movement and the stroke itself is merely shortened. The action still remains smooth and concerted. The time is quickened, but the rhythm is maintained. Of course, the length of the swing back to take a rising ball is reduced, but the force imparted to the ball will also be reduced, since the player will borrow from the extra speed of the rising ball to impart speed to the returning ball.

Pace begets pace. The inexperienced player, meeting drives of unfamiliar speed, is inclined to forget this fundamental canon. In many of his replies he must think of his own racket not as a battering ram but as a resilient shield against which the ball is hurled. The repercussion of the ball will itself be speedy. The young player has but to knock up against a wall to realise this elementary truth.

Economy of Effort.

The game of a player like Henri Cochet, which for this very reason appears so easy and effortless—a style at once simple and elusive—is largely composed of strokes which are only guards to the more forceful strokes of his opponent. Of relatively small stature, gaining nothing from his height or reach, this French champion is yet able, by the use of hip and shoulder rotation, to grade both the pace and direction of all his strokes, controlling each with great accuracy. His strength lies neither in his own arms nor legs, but in his thighs and shoulders ; by employing both to the very best advantage in the manner previously described, he obtains his wonderful results.

And this is why, there can be little doubt, Cochet (like Doherty before him) does not tire like ordinary mortals. Many of these are attempting to hit the ball every time, firstly as if the arm and the racket were the sole weapons at the disposal of the striker, and, secondly, as if the ball itself were motionless and " dead," needing, as it were, to have life whipped into it by an independent blow.

Mlle Lenglen's unexampled skill at lawn tennis was not due to any phenomenal strength of muscle or stamina ; she had neither. It was due, in the first place, to the rhythm or sequential movement of her stroke production, promoting perfect balance and timing, with an absence of strain on either wing ; in the second place, to a trained sense of anticipation which enabled her to reach the ball, wherever it pitched or was struck, in minimum time ; and, thirdly, to her intuitive practice of the principle that the pace of the oncoming ball could be used, without conscious exertion, to generate pace for the returned ball. By these qualities she held fatigue at bay. Her less enlightened or less endowed adversaries would appear to be making all the mistakes. It was their losing strokes rather than the winning strokes of Mlle Lenglen which seemed to be deciding the issue. Yet against players nearer their own class these opponents of the French champion would be making winning strokes all the time.

Doherty, Cochet, and Lacoste had the same power in their own epochs for the same reason. They were but vindicating style which comes from a rational comprehension of physical laws. By following their example and methods the student will find himself on rising ground.

Absence of Spin Strokes.

Incidentally he will find that none of these players, nor Mlle Lenglen, used under- or top-spin on their normal driving strokes. All of these masters of what may be termed the "sweeping" school, as distinct from the "hitting" school, presented an open racket-face to the ball, although all—and especially Lacoste, who had less genius, but more industry—induced spin, which assisted the controlled flight of the ball, by "closing" the face slightly as they followed through. They were and are "pure" stroke-makers, and it was the relatively spinless or flat drives of American masters like Tilden and R. N. Williams, although the first could employ at will every spin-stroke known to the game, which brought them to high eminence.

The theory and practice of super-spinning strokes receives some attention in the two succeeding chapters, which deal with the service and with volleying—strokes made before the ball has touched the ground. Even in these departments of the game their worship is to be deprecated. The battle of the cut or spin-invested stroke and the plain stroke has been fought in successive epochs; each time the latter has triumphed. It has won the day both on scientific and on physical grounds, because it has been proved that the style which produces the plain stroke can both outmanœuvre and outstay the style which produces the top- or under-spinning stroke.

For in the production of the latter, apart from the question of controlled speed, more labour is required from the limbs concerned; the physical strain is increased by the longer and less fluent movement; the danger of reaction is the greater. Mastery over the ball, and, therefore, in lawn tennis, is the fruit of strainless and straightforward stroke action. That action has become quicker as the game, both in attack and defence, has quickened, and as the youth and ardour of all nations have rallied to exploit it. But most of the standard strokes of Cochet were played by Renshaw and repeated by Doherty, and neither the champions of the past nor the champions of the present used, or found much difficulty in handling, the "breaking ball."

CHAPTER
SEVEN

THE ART AND PRACTICE OF THE SERVICE

CHAPTER SEVEN

THE ART AND PRACTICE OF THE SERVICE

THE service at lawn tennis has always intrigued the hand of man. The service has the proverbial advantage of a first blow ; the direction and pace may be controlled without reference to the opponent's racket. This prerogative has provoked enterprise through the various epochs. The first servers, borrowing their style from tennis, cut the ball with an underhand swing. As the net was then raised against them at the sides, the direction of their stroke was limited ; the flight of the ball was inclined to be stereotyped.

With the introduction of the overhead volley, chiefly by the Renshaw brothers, and the lowering of the net, both at the posts and in the centre, the overhead service began its more stimulating career. The earlier overhead services, even those of contemporary champions, were distinguished more for their accuracy of aim and variety of pace than for their destructive speed and exaggerated spin ; most of them were not intended to win the point outright. That this conception of their function did not satisfy a progressive world the Americans, Australians, and, for a time, the French did their best to demonstrate, and early in the twentieth century Wimbledon competitors were puzzled and to some extent paralysed by alien services with "googly" breaks.

Later, when these blows were found to have their limitations, came the faster and more menacing services of players like Brookes, Gobert, Tilden, and Patterson, all of whom, except Tilden, used them as artillery fire to mine a position afterwards stormed by the volleyer. Championships of long lineage were won by these services and their complements. But evolution was not arrested by their arrival. When modern players of the Doherty school developed their art of mobile defence and of extracting speed from the speed of their adversaries, standing well in over the baseline for their returns, the reign of the hurricane server was threatened; his fangs, as it were, were partially drawn.

These super-speed services remain, nor are they likely to disappear from a game which invites aggressive strokes and which would lose much of its appeal if they were not exploited. Modern implements and surfaces—rackets with stronger frames and implacable stringing, balls with smoothed, unstitched covers, fitted with air-retaining linings, and courts of firm, true, and resilient quality—minister to speed and cultivate it. But these improvements in equipment have also promoted precision and resource in the replies to the heavier blows. They have strengthened the work of the rapier as much as the work of the sword, developing volleying and half-volleying and those quickly-played strokes founded on the principle of repercussiom which the French exploit with much delicacy. As the reply to the super-fast service was developed on rational lines—and we have to thank an American [Mr. R. N. Williams] for pointing the way—its valuation was reviewed. Its stock as a match-winning asset was inclined to fall; its influence on physical reserves in a long match assumed a greater significance. Players with long memories, watching the quieter services of the French, began to ask themselves whether the services of the Doherty brothers, relatively of medium pace but always judiciously placed, were not as effective for victory and of greater scientific value than the thunderbolt deliveries, some of them swerving in the air, of their successors.

Invited to reflect on this conclusion, the reader who is seeking to acquire an efficient service, satisfying the laws of physics, may be directed to a method of instruction which endeavours to enumerate the principles outlined in the last two chapters. Whether, at a later stage, he elects to employ a medium-pace delivery, free from break, or to invest his service with arbitrary speed or spin, does not alter the essential movements necessary for the creation of power to strike the ball.

Grip of the Racket.

The majority of good servers hold the racket in the same way; the wisdom of the epochs in this respect has been handed down. René Lacoste's method of acquiring this standard grip may be recommended. "Place your racket flat on a table," he writes, "then put the hand on the racket as if to grasp it. Surround the handle with the fingers so that their extremities, without moving the racket, come in contact with the surface of the table. Then raise the racket with the left hand and, leaving your fingers in contact with the handle, close your hand. You will thus have an excellent grip which will enable you to execute at will the straight service, the American service, and the ordinary cut service." Some players extend the forefinger along the handle ; Lacoste prefers to keep all the fingers close together. The point is not material to efficiency, although it may be noted that players who are more powerful overhead than Lacoste find that the slightly raised forefinger gives them a greater last-second control of direction. This applies more particularly to tall men.

The Swing.

The physical action is in the nature of a swing, and since the player must remain more or less stationary while making the stroke, the analogy of a man swinging Indian clubs may be used. Indeed, if the learner would think in terms of the Indian-club movement, remembering that both hands are each swinging a club in sympathy, he would realise the important part played by the left (or non-striking) hand in the production of the service, and the need for its co-operative training.

In the service, as in club swinging, the two hands, arms, forearms, and shoulders should make similar movements simultaneously and in the same rhythm, sometimes in the same and sometimes in opposite directions. By creating and "feeling" these unified movements the server will acquire more balance and more power.

When the server is in the "ready" position he should begin the movement of swinging the racket with the right forearm by a little turning movement to the left (as in beginning to walk) of his upper-arm and shoulder. This will tend to move his right arm forward past his right leg ; at the same time his left hand holding the ball will swing as far back past his left leg. Then with the turning movement of the shoulders (as in the pendulum swing again) his right arm will swing backward and up, while his left arm will swing forward and up. If there is the same sympathetic action in the forearms as there has been in the shoulders, the left forearm can be raised with the ball to the level of the chin, when it should be released for the "throw-up." The right forearm is also carried up in order to allow the racket head to fall behind the left shoulder and thence behind the right—as in the twirl of the Indian-club exercises.

Both forearms will have moved in unison—that is the cardinal point. Next, both arms should be lowered below the elbows, which should always remain bent—the left after the ball has been released from the hand in the "throw-up," the right to permit the server to turn the arm which, if bent, will be controlled through the shoulders and hips for the forward motion of the service. The racket, having been whirled round behind the server's head with the help of the wrist, can then be made to travel upwards and forwards to meet the descending ball. The second circular swing is made with the right shoulder as its axis and with the power generated by the rotary motion of the two shoulders and by the speed of the racket completing its Indian-club movement.

Weight Distribution.

During the whole of the stroke the player's weight will be on his left or forward foot. Only thus can his balance be maintained and the "pedestal" kept firm; swaying of the body will be avoided, and the free movement of its upper part in the shoulders and upper arms be ensured. Moreover, a well-balanced left leg permits a truer "throw-up" of the ball and assists the accuracy and control of the whole service delivery.

Practice.

To acquire the "habit" of the synthetic movement described, it is not essential for the beginner to practise on a court or indeed out of doors. He may use any space under cover or in the open, wide and high enough to permit the swinging of his arms and the projection of the ball; a bare wall, draped to deaden the rebound, is a useful adjunct. At first he may rehearse the double-handed movements without either racket or ball; children should always be initiated in this way. Then the racket may be carried without the ball and *vice versa*; then both together. The impact of racket and ball need not be fast or violent at first. The beginner is not concerned in the early stages with pace and direction. His primary object is to acquire an easy and rhythmic swing; the subsequent behaviour of the ball may be considered later.

Throwing up the Ball.

The upward projection of the ball for the service—the only stage of the game when the player may actually "handle" it—is in itself a small yet important art. To launch the ball badly or carelessly is to invite a bad or careless service—in short, to present an advantage to the opponent before he has "entered the ring." In the synthetic swing already described the ball should be thrown up to such a height that its static stage (that point when gravitation pulls it down) corresponds exactly with the racket's impact. That means it should be hoisted not higher or lower than the highest point the player can reach with the centre of his racket. If it be thrown too high (a familiar fault, especially with tall players) the server will be striking a descending ball; the risk of imperfect timing and of controlled direction will be increased. If it be thrown too low the chance of a fault or faulty stroke is even greater.

The ball should be thrown up as nearly vertical as possible, for it should fall in the same straight line. Later on, of course, when the player develops strategy and guile, this rigidity in direction can be varied. The ball should be released with the palm pointing upwards and not downwards or sideways. Many women players have the fingers dipped towards the ground after the ball has gone—a sign that it has been projected badly, and often the cause of a curved throw and a defective service. The absolute tyro should not attempt to hold more than one ball in the hand. The match player will find two a sound average. To hold three may avoid collecting a duplicate if a "let" be called; but if the first service is good the other two balls have either to be carried or discarded—the first is not a wise habit and the second is a bad one. Some big-palmed servers have been known to carry five balls at once. Tilden, without recharging his hand, has served four aces and then—as a "curtain" to a *tour de force*—tossed over the fifth ball amiably to his victim. The novice will not even attempt such coups.

The Feet.

The position of the feet for the standard service is important, but not so crucial, I believe, as some instructors suppose. A natural and comfortable stance is better than a champion's stance slavishly copied. Broadly speaking, the left toes should be at rest about six inches behind the baseline and, from the right court, should point either straight along the line which the ball is to follow or a little to the right of it. The right foot should be slightly to the right of and about two feet behind the left. From the left court, if the same position is taken relatively to the flight of the ball, the right foot will be to the left of a line drawn through the left foot parallel to the side-lines.

The best servers, by which is meant those who control the direction and speed of their deliveries to the best advantage, rarely serve foot-faults. The creation of great pace by Tilden and Patterson involves an impulsion which necessitates a firm and definitely circumscribed foot action, although both may raise their heels. Lacoste, with his slower speed but greater accuracy of direction, varied at will, will pivot and turn on his toes ; but his left foot does not leave its base and his right does not swing over the line. It will be found indeed that the players whose services are most measured and whose marksmanship is most effective—players who deliberately aim at certain spots in the opposite court with malice aforethought—are the most "restful" (that is, the least precipitant) on their feet when serving. The Doherty brothers and W. M. Johnston were cases in point. Conversely, players of specialised or incomplete equipment—those who may mistrust their ground strokes and who may seek to conceal the fact by a hurried excursion to the net—are often foot-faulters, although they may not be conscious of the fact—they allow their feet to slip away from them. To the inveterate volleyer, of course, every second of time is precious ; yet at the height of the server-volleyer epidemic there were fewer foot-faulters than later, when this form of attack lost some of its appeal. The reason was probably twofold—a decreasing vigilance on the part of line-umpires due to the selection of less knowledgeable officials, and the fact that, with the spread of the game all over the world, less honour was paid by tournament players to the letter of a complex rule.

The position of the server in relation to the court's width has changed with the game's development. Common sense and science have both assisted evolution. In Major Wingfield's original hour-glass court, as we have seen, there was a special diamond-shaped pen within the court marked out for the server. It was not intended that he should do more than merely initiate an exchange. When, almost immediately—indeed very few pioneers remember the diamond marking—the server straddled the baseline with his feet, his blow, because of the variation in the net's height, was inevitably a slanting one ; he stood near the extremity of the baseline to make the diagonal underhand delivery.

The overhead service and the lowering of the net changed the orientation of the server. His command of the opposite court from the higher altitude increased ; he was able, so to speak, to spring down from aloft on what he hoped would be a more or less defenceless opponent. Naturally he shifted his base of operations towards the centre of the line, for as he came nearer it the length of his downward blow shortened. Moreover, his sense of "overlordship," of a moral and intellectual claim to penetrate his adversary's realm, was enlarged by the central position. He need move but little from his base to attack either court or either wing of that court ; and if he were coming in behind his service he had less distance to travel and a wider command of the net when he got there. The base, then, of all first-class servers is near the bisecting mark on either side. Some of them, indeed, are too near it, and commit a foot-fault by stepping into the territory behind the wrong court—a habit easily contracted and as easily overlooked.

The relationship between the first and second services, like most family relationships, can be smooth or vexing. They may be helpful to each other or mutually destructive. Thus it profits no server to deliver a first ball wildly into the net or out of court if his second ball be so coy and inoffensive by way of penance that the receiver can flog it for a winning ace. On the other hand, a first service that finds its mark, if less majestically than the server would desire, has two definite virtues—it stimulates the *amour propre* of the server, giving him greater confidence for the second stroke ; it conserves his energy.

Every fault, like every misdirected drive, promotes psychological as well as physical depression. The Dohertys rarely served a double fault, yet both were enterprising servers. Tilden, Johnston, Lacoste, and Mlle Lenglen, although their deliveries differ in production and effect, as rarely presented their opponents with an unearned stroke. The fact is that all these great players—four of the greatest lawn tennis has provided—served well within their physical powers. The service art in their hands was not exclusively an act of annihilation ; its main object was to embarrass the receiver. If he were mortally wounded, so much the better ; if he struck back, the server's blow had some influence on the character of the reply ; it placed the server in the best position to deal with it. Marksmanship rather than sheer velocity has been the attribute of all great servers. It is what the service does at the other end, where it pitches and hów it bounds, that matters ; its speed over the net is of less importance.

Lacoste has laid it down that " a good player should know thoroughly how to execute a straight service, a slice service, and an American service " [*Lacoste on Tennis*]. One would be inclined, reflecting on the teachings of forty years, to go farther and say that a player who has a perfect command of the first two, other things being equal, can aspire to and win championship honours. It is quite true that the American service has won high distinction in the past and is still employed with deadly effect against all who have not, by practice and brain, learnt to return it ; but while it must remain valuable on that account and will continue to be exploited, and while its use in doubles play has advantages which will be explained in a later chapter, it is not an essential equipment for a player otherwise fully armed.

The American Service.

Its origin, one does not forget, was more or less accidental. It was the creation of a volleyer [Mr. Holcombe Ward] anxious to get off the mark quickly in his rush to the net. Experimenting on a college court, this volleyer discovered that by hitting the ball with an upward swing of the racket both swerve and break were produced. The server, following through less elaborately, could swing his right foot over and into the court more rapidly ; the receiver was puzzled and discomfited by the unusual behaviour of the ball. Its novelty was disconcerting ; employed against the first British Davis Cup team which invaded America, its potency was almost that of the first " gas attack." But familiarity bred a certain measure of contempt. The ball had " check " ; it remained on court just long enough to be examined ; S. H. Smith's drive mastered it completely on British courts ; the Dohertys got on easy terms with it ; it has no terrors for the leading Frenchmen now.

All these heavily-breaked services (the American, the

reverse American, and other varieties) involve in their production a physical strain disproportionate to their value. They are undoubtedly useful as variants ; launched unexpectedly, as a forcing shot for a sudden volleying coup, they may win valuable points. But one agrees with Lacoste that "these services fail to pay in proportion to the preparation which they require and the risk which they render necessary."

Spin.

The distinction may be emphasised between spin which can be obtained by an easy, harmonious action and which has the virtue of bringing the ball into faster contact with the court after it has crossed the net, and spin of an exaggerated character which can only be produced by a complex and tiring movement and which, while yielding a "side-stepping" bound at the other end, is yet slow enough to offer an offensive reply to an agile opponent.

Lacoste and Johnston may be mentioned as servers who employ spin to the best strategic and physical advantage. Neither has the height of Tilden nor Patterson ; both have an action which is at once smooth and comfortable, yet favourable for the production of controlled spin. Allowing the left hand to dovetail with the right on the Indian club principle and launching the ball almost vertical, the American imparts spin by striking the ball from left to right, at its upper part, on the right side. As in Lacoste's case, the action promoting the spin is the outcome, not of any abnormal movement, but of the shoulder's rotation. The shoulder moves backwards in the preparation of the stroke and comes forward again at the moment of the ball's impact. Neither Johnston nor Lacoste, it should be noted, is in any way "shaken" by the gyration ; they preserve perfect balance throughout the whole movement.

The Cannon-ball Service.

The so-called cannon-ball service is an affair of strong and tall men—strong, because the cumulative strain on the firer is considerable and can only be resisted by powerful physiques ; and tall, because, bearing in mind that only a limited portion of the opponent's court is "targetable" from the baseline, a missile launched from a high base (in Tilden's case as high as nine feet) must have an obvious advantage. Very few servers can command these two factors.

Express services, of course, depend as much on rhythm and balance as slower deliveries. There is nothing " freakish " about the withering services of Tilden and Patterson ; their authors are masters of a practical craft. Both bend the arms more than the average server ; both make great use of the forearm and the wrist. Tilden begins and completes his stroke with a bent arm ; the illusion is, indeed, created in the minds of some onlookers that the arm is not stretched out to its full height when the ball is struck. It does not require a slow-motion picture to remove this fallacy. Tilden's arm, tightening as he rises on his toes, is released like a spring, mounting almost to the vertical line ; he employs every inch of his height to achieve the downward blow. With Patterson the delivery is more measured, the loins are more relaxed in preparation, the forward flexion of the body more pronounced. His service has more dipping spin than Tilden's ; it can be as destructive, but in a long match is not so well controlled ; it breeds more double faults. This is because he flexes and tires the wrist more ; and, of course, following in much more frequently to volley, he exposes the forearm and wrist muscles to the greater strain.

For their spectacular effect, their influence on the game's drama, these super-fast services must always claim the respect of galleries. The crowd will always applaud the knock-out blow. But their efficacy as point-winners has been modified by the enterprise and agility of their " receivers." The alert and studious French, practising their art on covered courts, have developed the " blocking " return into a fine art. Thus one " spectacle " is followed by another—to the enlivening of lawn tennis.

CHAPTER
EIGHT

VOLLEYING VARIATIONS

CHAPTER EIGHT

VOLLEYING VARIATIONS

YOUTHFUL players of lawn tennis to-day are always surprised to hear that the first champion at Wimbledon [in 1877] was a volleyer. Nor was his volley a mere pat over the net. Spencer W. Gore had a natural aptitude for all ball games; in the rackets court at Harrow and elsewhere his nimble footwork, long reach, flexible wrist, and quick eye—the essentials, then as now, of a good volleyer—had shone in good company. When pursuing the relatively new game of lawn tennis, what more natural than that he should go up to the net and, with a dexterous turn of a strong wrist, volley the drives of his opponents? The stroke may have been novel in its conception and in its effect; obviously it vindicated the first great principle of lawn tennis, which was to force the opponent away from his base. Spencer Gore was, of course, favoured by the net's height at that time. He could not very well be passed on the wings, for the net at the posts was five feet high. He had but to entrench himself near the centre, which was eighteen inches lower, to intercept the main stream of drives; and the lob had not then been discovered, although next year, when he defended his title, this ruse was to prove his undoing.

No doubt, coming from rackets, with its hard ball, the first champion found the soft ball of lawn tennis an inviting medium for the volleyer's art. His successors, the Renshaws, were to demonstrate that its relative lightness and elasticity offered to the nimble and mobile player a greater variety of volleying strokes than any other game. In no other is it possible to do so much with the ball at full pitch. Hence the universal popularity of the volley, its wide appeal to player and onlooker alike, its scope for enterprise, daring, and resource. Lawn tennis can be enjoyed without its use; great players like Tilden and Mlle Lenglen, for strategic reasons, have won great singles matches without volleying once; but if the volley had never been invented (or had been penalised out of existence, as some of the earliest baseliners actually suggested), the game must have lost its savour and possibly its life as well.

Like the service and the drive, the volley has passed through an orderly evolution ; even more has its development responded to improvement in surface and equipment and to the more intensive footwork which both have provoked.

As suggested in the previous chapter the speeding-up of the service has tended, in modern championship play, not to send the receiver farther away from the net, but to bring him nearer in. In sympathy with this forward movement, which anticipates a sterner frontal attack, the normal driving base of many arduous players has also been advanced. They have come forward to meet the ball rather than to await its coming ; they return it on its rise and not on its fall. The tendency has been to play more strokes within the actual boundaries of the court, less in the " surround." This is not exactly a new passion. The agile Renshaw twins exploited it ; some of the Americans and Norman Brookes warmed to it ; it has remained for the post-war Frenchmen to reveal its fuller possibilities.

This disposition to play more ground strokes nearer the net (those strokes, that is, which lend themselves to an advanced position) has naturally widened the scope and practice of the volley, and not only of the standard volley which is played from a winning position, adequately prepared. The forecourt, which was used freely by the Renshaws (when the attack was admittedly less violent) and also by Brookes, most skilful at " clearing " his feet when running in, has received much more strategic attention generally from youthful and quick-footed players. To watch Cochet at work in this area (some of it forbidden territory by text-book law) is to watch an exponent of what appears to be a natural and co-ordinated art, pursued with the confidence of orthodoxy. The half-volley—an emergency stroke for most first-class players—becomes an attacking shot in the hands of the Frenchman ; the drive-volley, another difficult stroke, flowers into a commonplace ; drop, stop, hook, and other delicate volleys are executed either forehand or backhand with an easy facility.

The volleys of Cochet and Borotra, and in less measure of Vincent Richards, the American, differ in two respects from the volleys of the older school, although some members of the latter were their superiors in other strokes. The first is that the "new" volleyer is battling against strokes of greater speed and a greater variety of spin than his predecessors; he is required to be more alert, more daring, and more resourceful. The second is that, by virtue of the increased speed in all departments of the game, the forward movement, if it is to reap its reward, has to be made at a greater pace. The player, in short, must enter the race with the ball, accelerating his own movements with its quicker and more varied flight. In this competition he must be prepared to acquire and employ, not strokes which are new in architecture, but strokes which are new in their rapid sequence and effect. It follows that mobility of body and mind, flexibility of foot and wrist (indeed of toes and fingers), and a capacity to blend force with finesse at discretion, are required by the modern volleyer.

Volleying Practice.

The novitiate will not, of course, expect to soar at once into the rarified atmosphere of the champion. He must learn to walk before he can hope to run, but he will do well to cultivate volleying at the earliest possible stage. Actually it is the easier department for private practice, because it does not require the space demanded by the bounding ball; any smooth wall, in or out of doors, and enough room to turn in, are alone necessary. Moreover, the eye will be trained to the sense of rapid exchange, the feet will learn their dove-tailing movements in less time, if the "terror" of the opposing player is withdrawn—if the silent and accommodating wall returns, without break or other sly device, the ball that is aimed at its wide and friendly frontage. Do not then neglect this wall "knock-up"; many a tyro has developed under its secret protection, many a champion has regained confidence through its agency.

The simpler volleys, those of waist height, will naturally be learnt first. Here the player who has learnt to bend the arms in preparation for the drive will have an advantage; he will find the quick parry with the racket, its head above the wrist, the easier to achieve. The learner will be facing the wall (or net) instead of turning to the right or left of it as in the case of the drive; the shoulder will consequently turn much less, the elbow will often press the side; the wrist will often be the shield of resistance and the generator of force. The wrist, in fact, will assume the functions of a " little arm " ; its flexion will be of great importance ; its capacity to tighten under impact and to loosen after impact found to be decisive. For if the follow-through of the arm, which is essential after the volley, is to be denied the impetus of the swing back, as it often must be, the challenge to the wrist must necessarily be more severe ; upon its strength and resilience will depend the success of the stroke. Time is the essence of the contract in volleying ; the shorter wrist can often succeed where the longer arm would fail.

Footwork in Volleying.

Fluent footwork, it need hardly be said, is fundamental to good volleying. For some of the deep-court drives the player may be more or less " anchored," having time and space for an elaborate swing. In making the volley both these conditions are restricted and may be reduced to a minimum ; the preparation cannot be as long. Since the shoulder line will sometimes be parallel to the net when the ball is struck, sometimes at right angles to it, and sometimes turned completely round so that the player is facing his own baseline, the normal driving stance will not serve the volleyer, except when the ball is conveniently placed. The opponent's mission will be to " wrong-foot " the volleyer ; the surge of play may not permit him to plant the feet firmly. Therefore he must be prepared to execute many strokes from a quickly improvised, sometimes from a technically untenable, base ; his feet must be the loyal and obedient servants of a quick brain.

Roughly speaking, the big drivers, the players employing long artillery, are the big " striders " ; they need room for the swing of their arms and legs. The best volleyers, those of most versatility, are players of short steps. Thereby they readjust the shifting balance the better ; their equilibrium is not as often threatened by the body's momentum, moving, as it were, against the ball. The best French volleyers are all short-striding ; so are the best Americans and the best Australians. H. L. Doherty was a typical instance ; the short, " pattering " steps of Roper Barrett and C. P. Dixon in the region of the net helped to make them the great volleyers they were. Best of all is the player who can alternate the leap with the pirouette as occasion and position may require. Mlle Lenglen and Jean Borotra are cases in point, and there can be little doubt that both won many of their triumphs by ability to employ at will the longest and the shortest stride.

But if net and back-court play demand their own footwork to suit the different positions of the body, the same principles of physical balance are in force. Nature cannot be cheated of her claims. She demands that the feet shall be placed in such a way that the movements of the trunk and arms above them do not strain an anatomy which, if properly trained, will respond to almost every emergency. It is just as necessary, as in driving, when making the normal forehand volley to advance the left foot, and in making the normal backhand volley to advance the right foot ; and for those shoulder-high volleys, executed from floating balls on either wing, it is just as essential that the shoulder-turn should govern and control the follow-through and that power should pass up through the thighs, balanced and turning on the legs.

The question of balance is even more vital in volleying than in driving. In the former there is less time, sometimes only a minimum of time, to recover it. The shots which often surprise the opponent most are not those of great speed or even of unexpected angle ; they are those which look to be impossible of achievement because the body of the volleyer appears as if it cannot recover position in time.

It is, therefore, the preservation of balance for making the next stroke which constitutes the hardest problem for the learner. It may be solved partly by watching expert volleyers in court, partly by remembering that, in the region of the net, the shorter the step the better will the feet dovetail to permit a sequential balance. Even when called upon to make strokes which seem to be quite unorthodox—those, for example, with the back turned to the net—the well-balanced volleyer can, by a swift flanking movement, recover poise for the next blow.

The Hold of the Racket.

The question of the racket hold must always concern the quality and completeness of the volleying art. There have been great volleyers who, because of their early training, used the same face of the racket for both forehand and backhand strokes. The fingers of Norman Brookes were in front of the handle and facing the net for the latter ; and for his inimitable push volleys, distributed at will to any section of the court, he undoubtedly gained time and did not appear to lose in control. W. M. Johnston, although employing the Western grip for his backhand, was able to produce both speed and spin, to the embarrassment of nearly all his adversaries. Yet the experience of successive epochs was against these great players. In the technical sense neither was completely equipped. The grip they employed on the backhand, which did not reverse the racket face, was a weakness under pressure in the deep backhand corner with a low ball, because the raised elbow which it involved did not provide adequate freedom for the swing back and the follow-through. They protected themselves from assault in this quarter under a physical strain. The defect might be concealed from the onlooker and from nearly every opponent by the strategic brilliance of their attack ; they gained their triumphs in spite of it.

The Backhand Volley.

In the production of the backhand volley the learner may be advised to follow the structural methods of the Dohertys, Mlle Lenglen, Cochet, and Lacoste. They may differ in degree ; the rational principle is the same ; they are armed for every emergency. By reversing the racket face they conform to orthodoxy and vindicate pure style ; by allowing the back of the hand to face the net they widen the range of power, broadening the racket's sweep ; by bending the knees and lowering the whole trunk they are able to achieve the lateral volley as smoothly near the ground as away from it. More, they are able to screen their body, and to produce more than a merely defensive stroke, even when the ball is hurled at them at close range. Their racket hold (the strength of the lateral vice) is both a shield and a " shock-absorber " ; without any change of principle they can play strokes near their body or away from it. And the resources of repercussion, mentioned in a previous chapter, can best be exploited, thus conserving precious energy.

Variety of Strength & Depth.

To command graded strength as well as graded length must be the ambition of the progressive volleyer. He cannot be a complete master of the court, or feel that he is climbing towards that pinnacle, until he can mix the plain and deep volley (which he will use more often) with the volley which carries " check," the product of spin. As in the driving strokes, the student will avoid the habitual cultivation of spin lest it becomes a fetish with him and his volleys lose the finality which his previous strategy has earned. The deep and honest volley may well give him a quicker decision ; and the fact should never be forgotten that every volley which requires " draw " also requires a turn of the wrist to execute it. The cumulative effect of these repeated " stabs " will be to tire the arm for the basic strokes farther back in the court.

The Drop Volley & the Stop Volley.

Yet the production of the drop and stop volley, performed on either wing and at the shortest notice, will be needed by every complete player. It can so frequently be made the " holing out " shot. Without them the game would lose one of its happiest refinements and the player his full meed of joy. " Slice " and " chop " are often used synonymously to describe a spin-fed volley. The terms may be separated here to mean, in the case of a slice, a ball that is volleyed with under-spin, which checks its career, and, in the case of the chop, a ball that is struck with over-spin which tends to make it shoot forward on touching the ground. Some players will use the one more than the other, and *vice versa* ; some, the least prudent, will use either to the total exclusion of the more straightforward volley ; the few, and they will be the masters, will select either or reject both at discretion, as the situation may demand.

The position of the ball in relation to the player and of both to that of the opponent must obviously be the determining factor. A ball near the net that can only be reached when it is dropping, will need, like the mashie shot at golf, the assistance of an inclined racket face, causing it to rise again ; and if it is not to rise too high or to bound too generously it will also need a slanting blow as well. This is a delicate shot, inviting disaster if the timing be faulty ; but it may be wooed and won by patient practice and the friendly aid of a common wall. So may the even more difficult hook-volley taken—sometimes *in extremis*—with the back turned towards the net. Borotra, Cochet, Richards, and Tilden (on the backhand) are adept at this shot. It is more of a stab than a stroke ; it should only be attempted under provocation.

The Half-Volley.

The half-volley is a familiar stroke. Its description, as any slow-motion picture will prove, is a misnomer. The ball is not actually struck with the racket touching, nor even nearly touching, the court; the impact in all cases is several inches above it. The illusion, greater to the onlooker than to the player, although often held by him, is due to the elliptic flights in opposite directions of the racket and the ball and of their appearing to collide on the court itself. But the ball is actually rising when it meets the racket; not otherwise would the returning ball obtain its velocity both from the momentum of the racket and its own repercussion. The half-volley has been described as a poor relation; it does not deserve that implied disparagement. Commanded by a time-saving aggressor it can be employed, even at the back of the court, with conspicuous success. Señorita de Alvarez has broken through a driving attack with its sudden application; and she can play it on the backhand with a top-spin that adds to its surprise. The half-volley is likely to be exploited much more in the modern game. The ambitious may be advised to cultivate it—when they have learned the standard strokes, the drive, and the volley.

The Overhead Volley.

The overhead volley is as old as the first championship meeting; its development has been nearly as progressive. Wimbledon crowds (relatively small, but none the less discerning) applauded the "Renshaw smash" in the 'eighties, hailing it as the *coup de grâce*; modern throngs in England and overseas have cheered the overhead "kills" of Dwight Davis (one of the fiercest left-handed blows), McLoughlin, Patterson, Gobert, Lycett, Borotra, and Cochet.

Modern smashing, like other punitive strokes, has no doubt gained in speed and decision by the evolution of rackets and balls; but not every famous overhead player is, or has been, a famous server, and the analogy between the two strokes is not as complete as many people suppose. Indeed, the general quickening in footwork which has characterised the last decade has induced many of the more agile players to cultivate the smash with both feet off the ground, thus reducing the efficacy of the lob and narrowing the area of what has been called the "danger zone." Nor is overhead play as definitely associated with maximum force. Finesse implies restraint as well as rigor; the angle of the overhead volley can be as important as its speed; delicate strokes in the forecourt, with or without spin, sliced and chopped, have been developed as finishing thrusts, feeding alert minds as well as strong muscles.

The service analogy is, however, true in the sense that good servers can usually smash well. They have acquired the requisite rhythm which does not disturb the balance, coming up from the feet to the arms, when the head is raised above its normal "net" outlook. Inveterate drivers (and the majority of women players may be so described) are not, as a rule, good overhead, because their line of vision, like their line of stroke, is more or less lateral; their stance and swings are regulated for the low, long shots.

Smashing is essentially a matter of correct timing—of watching and waiting. Greater vigilance and measurement are necessary for two reasons—the first, because a lofted ball has less "life" and will require a firmer and more deliberate blow to rekindle its speed; and the second because, by a relative pause, the smasher will have time (when he is trained to notice such important things) to govern the direction of the smash by his opponent's position, which will rarely be static. Marksmanship in smashing is as vital as marksmanship in service; it is at once a point-winner and an energy saver.

The employment of greater deliberation to strike the slower-moving ball also gives time for the racket's face to be turned so that, when it is swung aloft, it is almost at right angles to the net. An assumption of the normal backhand hold will provide this preparation. Then, as the ball is struck, the wrist will turn the face to meet the ball, which it will strike, still at an inclined angle, thereby creating spin which will assist its direction and control. This, of course, is a reproduction of many service actions, but the player will not have the same influence over the flight of the objective in the smash as he will have in the service; there will be greater risk of disaster.

The more acrobatic player will sometimes hit the ball very far behind the head, leaping up from the court with both feet raised to execute the stroke. Temporarily he will have lost the fulcrum for his leverage, which is the ground; the resistance point for the "shock" will be transferred to his chest and shoulders. But he can quickly regain the essential balance for the next stroke—if there is to be one. The violence of the racket and arm movements in making the stroke will cause his legs to be drawn up, but the back part of his body will act as a counterpoise.

Just after the stroke is made the body will straighten itself; the player will come to earth with undisturbed balance, ready for action. But he will need to have been well balanced for the first stroke—that is, balanced by sequential and rhythmic movement. The ball may be struck in many unusual attitudes (indeed, will need to be in the course of a fast "all court" match) and the balance retained, if the sovereign principles of a natural and normal style have been grasped.

Some reference to the volleying methods of Jean Borotra may be added. This French player, in spite of (or, as may be suggested, because of) an unorthodox style, has revealed like none other the potentialities of the net attack based on speed of foot, serpentine agility, and incisive thrusts. Borotra's unorthodoxy lies in the fact that both for the forehand and backhand volley the racket handle is "palmed" so that not more than a quarter-turn provides him with the same leverage on either wing. The ball is pushed rather than hit, but so great is his speed of foot, with such agility can he turn without upsetting his balance, that he is forward enough to make the downward blow, bringing the weight of his own spring behind the ball. Thus he needs a minimum swing-back; his wrist is the great shock-resister and, when turned, the creator of direction and slice. While less mobile players are required to volley up and, therefore, to generate more force, he can lean on the ball, using his whole body, so to speak, as his "arm."

Yet even with his wonderful powers of bending and tacking, Borotra's game has the limitation of its own virtues. Because of his individual style he can never be the complete player in the technical sense that Lacoste, Cochet, and Tilden are, and that the Dohertys were. That fact will distress neither Borotra nor his generation. Technique alone does not win lawn tennis matches or even extract all that is exhilarating from the game. The virtues of speed, courage, enterprise, and tactical acumen which Borotra expresses may well provide the student with inspiration.

With the tactical problems presented by the conflict between baseline and volleying play, or of a combination of both in turn, future chapters will attempt to deal.

CHAPTER
NINE

TACTICS IN SINGLES

CHAPTER NINE

TACTICS IN SINGLES

SUCCESS in the singles art must depend on the ratio of ambition. A man may seek nothing higher (or, from his point of view, nothing lower) than a talent which will enable him to engage his neighbour in a friendly duel on his own lawn. He will only desire to play well enough to challenge his own body to physical exertion—enough to bring a comforting relaxation at its close. Were his standard to be superior to that of his opponent, this wish might not be gratified ; for lawn tennis is a game of exchange and derives its pleasure from effective barter. If the scales are weighted down too deeply on one side there can be no movement.

If, perhaps because of limitations at home, the player wants to spread his wings in the direction of the local club, or beyond it to that of its rival, he will probably need to raise his game to a higher level. His ratio will change with his environment ; so will his idea of lawn tennis values. Strokes that were winners on the home lawn may become losers on a foreign court. In discovering this fact tribulation may follow. But the mood of depression will be beneficial if it provokes greater application to the technique of the game and a determination to acquire additional strokes. Under the influence of sterner competition, equipment should be strengthened and a higher standard attained. Until a player explores its hidden caverns he cannot estimate the possible treasures of the game, nor test its maximum challenge to body and mind.

From club to tournament play is an easier journey, for there are all classes of events open to the competitor. The danger will be a possible retrogression, since the average quality of play may be below a level to encourage a forward movement. Competition is good for the soul, but sham fights against inferior adversaries are worse training than a private game on a club court.

From the tournament court to the championship or

international arena is, of course, a more hazardous passage. Yet the game in this rarer atmosphere will not differ materially from the game on the plane below. It will be faster and keener, the ball in transit may wear a more sinister aspect, the wiles of the opponent may appear more puzzling, the need for stricter training be more insistent. But there will be stimulating attributes—a better playing surface, an incentive to increased ardour, and the presence of spectators, which ought to provoke greater concentration.

In the reflections which follow on singles tactics it is assumed that the player has passed beyond what may be termed without offence—for, of course, many high-grade matches are played on private courts—the " common or garden " stage; that the player has acquired qualities of hand, heart, and head which entitle him to compete in an open tournament. And perhaps the non-tournament player may find them of some value. For if a man is intelligent enough to play the game tolerably well he will be intelligent enough to realise the value of education based on experience.

It has been well said by a champion of two hemispheres [R. Lacoste] that in order to win a lawn tennis match a player must be both a good soldier and a good general at the same time. Neither, of course, is the product of one season's practice, nor can the second rôle be assumed before the first. The requisites of the second are a complete equipment of sound strokes and a knowledge, gained by experience, of the best position on the battlefield for their most effective use.

Generalship.

Generalship implies a faculty for co-ordinating, controlling, and directing the forces at command, for so distributing and functioning them that victory may be achieved at the earliest moment. The importance of the last requirement may be emphasised; for a successful issue to the combat in hand cannot be the climax of ambition. The physical condition of the player at the close of one match may have a bearing on his chances in the next. The sooner he can compass the defeat of his adversary the longer interval will he have for recuperation. In other words, a " quick " victory in the first match by the best generalship may beget a quick victory in the second; to dally with Fate, even if immediate disaster be avoided, is to offer a hostage to fortune.

Before the science of tactics can be applied, accuracy both of aim and positional movement must be cultivated ; there must be unconscious efficiency in each. Mind and body must be working in liaison ; reflex action must be more or less automatic. Any plan of campaign, whether rehearsed or improvised, must fail if the forces necessary for its success cannot be summoned at will. Perfect coups can be worked out on paper ; their achievement on court is contingent on strokes executed from positions not always selected by design.

When a player possesses the requisite instruments of warfare he may turn profitably and whole-mindedly to a study of the tactical art. He will probably find that his researches and progress will be in direct ratio to the opportunity offered for match play. If there are several ways of executing a stroke effectively—that is, to obtain a given result—there are infinitely more ways of conducting a match in order to obtain victory or to minimise defeat. It is the selection of the best way that presents a problem at once difficult and attractive.

The choice of action will depend on varied factors. Not the least will be the calibre, methods, and mentality of the opponent. This aspect may be considered first, leaving to a later chapter such subsidiary factors as the condition of the court, the incidence of wind or rain, and the effect of climatic conditions on physical reserves.

It may be suggested that no player can hope to reach the eminence of the world's "First Ten" until he has an opportunity of meeting most of the other nine, and the provision may be applied to every other grade right down the scale. Skill and ardour may prove triumphant against lesser antagonists ; a player cannot measure his own capacity until a searching test has been applied. Even the average player will surprise himself by achieving new strokes when they are extracted by the strokes of a superior opponent. He will not be able to gauge his own latent resources until they are revealed by conflict. This, of course, is why the standard of the game, even at the top, has been steadily advancing. Explorers have been at work in all parts of the world ; at a big tournament they analyse each other's discoveries. New ideas are assimilated with old, one generation borrows from the last, the strain is rarified. A casual spectator may see nothing of this silent refinement ; the partisan of a past epoch may even doubt its existence ; yet evolution is steadily at work.

The Return of Service.

James Braid once declared that if he could see a man play his second shot he could estimate the standard of his golf. The service return has a similar relation to "form" in lawn tennis. Upon its direction, speed, and strength sometimes upon its spin, may depend the character of the rally and its length, and very often of its issue as well. In doubles, by reason of "third parties," the serving side must retain a presumptive advantage over the receiving side; in singles, under modern conditions, that advantage may be more psychological than real. The server, until the impact of the racket with the ball, is anchored to his base; from that fixed position he must generate the impulsive force. From his less restricted base the receiver will not be handicapped in the same way; he can be, if he chooses, nearer the net than his opponent and, therefore, nearer the spear-head of the attack.

The learner will not suppose that all services lend themselves to a forward-moving stance; the server may require him to leap to either side or may beat him outright. But these destructive deliveries involve both risk and strain. Nor are they best handled, as the French and some of the Americans have proved, from a "retiring" base. Borotra and Johnston have stood just inside the baseline to meet them, Cochet and R. N. Williams as far in as eight feet. The "blocking" return will, of course, need agile footwork and a quick eye. The gain of time and territory is material; it can be made even more valuable if a stride forward follows the impact of the racket with the ball. If the "blocked" return to a fast service be skilfully played—that is, with the counter speed that its own velocity invites—the server may be placed on the defensive at the earliest possible stage.

The Forward Base.

Whether he stands inside the baseline or outside it to receive the first service, the player should move forward to meet the slower and less menacing second. The risk of being trapped by a fast second should be taken. The server faces more risk in delivering a double fault; as a rule he will play for safety, especially if the point is deemed to be vital. And if the server, offering a breaking ball by way of variety, should elect to follow it to the net he will, if the receiver be well back, waiting for a falling ball, have the longer time to entrench himself.

The student of the modern game cannot be too strongly urged to cultivate a forward base for the service return. Oversea players at Wimbledon owed much of their success in the championships in the decade following the War to their strategic position in the court for handling the service. A famous Australian invader lost his only singles match in England in 1919 because his British opponent [P. M. Davson *v.* G. L. Patterson in the final of the covered court championship at Queen's] stood nearer in than any of his other rivals of that year.

Nature of the Return.

As to the character of the service return (its direction and speed) the player will soon discover that his success or failure as a singles exponent will depend on this fundamental phase of tactics. Just as it is the function of the server so to launch his service that, either by speed or placing, he may retain the initiative, it must be the object of the receiver to thwart this desire at the earliest opportunity. He will best do so if his return is in itself of the nature of a challenge—not necessarily, be it understood, a challenge of pace.

Lawn tennis is much more a science of graded strokes, of a decisive positional advantage gained by variation of length and strength, than it is a mere exchange of punitive blows. The lightness and resilience of a hollow rubber ball, coated with felt, offers a greater variety of stroke play than any other ball game. The discovery of this fact by the Renshaws transformed the long "rest" into the short "rest," ended the monotony of the baseline exchange, and revealed the potentialities of the volleying art. Lawn tennis had its lean years again, but only when back-court play appeared to be dominating the court. When youth moved its base forward there was, in effect, a Renshaw renaissance, a cosmopolitan acceptance of the "all-court" game.

A soft answer is credited with the virtue of checking wrath. The precept is not intended to preach surrender; it counsels control. One may, therefore, suggest that the most judicious reply to a fast service is not always a fast drive. The receiver's motto should be position rather than power; he must be playing for a future rather than a present coup. Therefore he will be advised to make his first return more of a "sounding" than a "storming" shot, remembering that before he can acquire controlled speed he must have steadiness of aim. The direction of the return should depend more on the methods of the opponent than on those of the receiver; and the quickest way to find these out in order to counter them is to vary the direction of the early service returns. The character and effect of the server's reply may reveal his policy; until that is ascertained and its strength gauged, his opponent cannot formulate his tactics.

Restraint of First Stroke.

A defensive reply may be the only possible reply to the service; an aggressive reply is not necessarily the best reply to an easier ball. There is always a liability of error over the first ground stroke; neither the mind nor the body may be "warmed up," and the wide choice of field (wider than at any other period of the rest) may and often does provoke indecision or carelessness. The reason why H. L. Doherty or Mlle Lenglen so rarely lost the point on the service return (that is, by netting the ball or hitting it out of court) was that, as an habitual rule, it was a restrained stroke; control and purpose were its main properties.

The tactical student may be advised to consider the court as a big outdoor chess-board. His ultimate object will be to checkmate his opponent, but he cannot hope to reach that conclusion in the first move. He must, therefore, manœuvre him into a position on the board which enables him to call "check." Strokes, like pieces, have their relative value in achieving this design; if the wrong one is used (if a "castle" or "bishop" be moved before a pawn) the strategic opportunity may be lost.

Major Tactics.

Reflecting on these lines, some consideration may be given to profitable tactics, as practised by masters, under varying conditions. By "masters" one means all-round and "all-court" players, not men who have made their name, nor who may have much to teach, as drivers or volleyers. For while these specialists have assisted in the evolution of the game and are, therefore, to be honoured, they have revealed at one time or another the defects of their good qualities, and confirmed the view that the best and quickest way to learn the art of lawn tennis is to gain confidence in the use of every stroke and not to practise one at the expense of the other.

Tactics against a Baseline Player.

A well-equipped player must naturally have a less difficult task against a baseliner than against a volleyer, even if the former has a superior ground speed at his command. For if he can so grade the strength and length of his own ground strokes, using the short cross-drive and the drop as a decoy, the baseliner is drawn into alien territory. His preference for a regular base, to which he can return more or less automatically, is ingrained ; it should be the object of his opponent to require him to leave it. It is easier to upset a long driver by removing his base than by driving through him, for the latter expedient involves more risk and more fatigue. The former plan, by opening the court either for a deep drive or for a volley, will tend to shorten the rally, since the baseliner will be deprived of the security of his stronghold.

Several players use under-spin in attempting to thwart the powerful baseliner. Spin is a useful servant but a bad master ; its tactical value is limited. Doherty, Cochet, and Mlle Lenglen did not employ it ; Lacoste used it sparingly in driving ; Tilden found it unprofitable against the French all-court masters, however effective it may have proved against less versatile opponents. A " cut " volley may sometimes be the best stroke for a decisive coup ; a " cut " drive is not a classic stroke and its value has been exaggerated. Its habitual use will tend to cramp a player's freedom and, because of its slower flight, place its author at the mercy of an alert volleyer or even at that of a double-winged driver.

Tactics against a Volleyer.

The tactics of an all-court player against an inveterate volleyer will depend upon the violence of the attack and its effect on the physical resources of the aggressor. Before the " googly " service was mastered (while its novelty lasted, that is), its authors would come in behind it every time ; and the rallies as a rule were short enough for the strain on stamina to be borne. But now a persistent net attack (without an interval for recuperation) cannot be maintained over a whole match. Borotratic volleying is not a five-set affair ; its efficiency lies in its periodical application.

The driver can always find room in the singles court to pass the volleyer if he can first find room to execute the passing shot. It need not necessarily be a clean pass; it should be a shot so aimed that even if the volleyer can reach it his power to make a decisive reply is reduced to a minimum. As a rule, volleyers are stronger on their backhands than on their forehands; the construction of the stroke gives them a wider range of control—that is, if they use the hold commended in a previous chapter. The experienced volleyer in planning his coups will rely on the tendency of the driver to play his ground strokes to this wing. It is more prudent under pressure to attempt the pass on the volleyer's forehand side; it is the lesser of two risks with a lofted ball.

The volleyer, unlike the back-court driver, will always be thinking in angles; he must, therefore, be countered on a geometrical basis. The volleyer will require a certain elevation to make his most effective downward blows, and by agility and anticipation he may yet obtain his "pedestal" even if the passing shot takes the widest path. The way is thus pointed to the foot and head line rather than to the waist line. The foot line will always prove more profitable, unless it is seen that the volleyer's momentum will carry him so far forward towards the net that the head line will give him a certain winner.

The volleyer's trade is to hit down; his raw material, so to speak, are waist- and shoulder-high drives; and by his tactics he will invite his opponent to feed him with these shots. The player must, therefore, elude him by "dipping" or lobbing. In regard to "dipping," remember that most volleyers are better at achieving half- or hook-volleys on the backhand than on the forehand—except those players (and there are many) who have a defective backhand grip which will resent a low ball dropping on their left side as they are running in. The observant player will have discovered this weakness if it exists.

The lob, of course, may be used both in defence and in attack. Its function in the former is to relieve a pressure that would otherwise be fatal, to recover positional freedom after tactical entanglement. The height of the lob (when discretion is possible) may be less important than its direction; for if a lob is high enough to elude the volleyer, even if he jumps to reach it, it must be a better lob if it falls to the ground in minimum time. There is nothing more demoralising to the persistent net player than to find that the *volte face* imposed on him cannot possibly retrieve the situation ; and when a man is running away from the net after running towards it, his double excursion, divided by a quick turn, is a useful aid to physical and psychological depression, which are closely allied.

Tactics against Lobbing.

Used as a complement to the drop shot, the lob can be most effectively employed in singles. The device in skilful hands can break and render nugatory a powerful attack. Beals Wright and Roper Barrett, neither an aggressive driver, were two of its masters ; they decoyed many a young player, even of Davis Cup rank, to his doom. The tactic can only be defeated by steadiness and circumspection, and by a concentrated effort to force the plotter to the back of the court and into a position where a counter-volleying attack will succeed. Counter pawkiness will not alone suffice, for if it comes to a battle of wits the man who has practised the coup assiduously will have an advantage, if the pace of the game is reduced on both sides.

The falling point of the lob should be regulated by the opponent's position and his relative strength on either wing. An ambitious learner may spend a very profitable afternoon in practising lobs from the baseline and its neighbourhood ; he may throw up the ball to get the requisite bound. There was one famous player who learnt to drive in this way. His target was always the opposite baseline ; as he gained proficiency with the high, slow lob, so he reduced the arc and increased the speed, still aiming for the same spot.

Tilden, it may be added here, had his own method for insuring fluent footwork when forced to run for a wide ball on his forehand. When he was about six feet away from the ball he made a little " skip step " that turned his body sideways to the net and brought his left foot towards the ball with an advance of his right ; he was in a position to make his stroke at once. His follow-through pulled his body round ; at the end of the swing he was once more facing the coming return. The blending of the short skip with the long was one of Tilden's secrets in extricating himself from losing positions.

Psychology.

Lacoste has made the sound point that, apart from his execution, the player should analyse his physical and intellectual resources and use them to develop his own game. Tactics, in short, cannot be imposed by text-book law ; they must be adapted to suit the personality of the individual.

The successful singles player must, therefore, be a student of psychology. The mind, like the body, has its reflex movements ; upon the relative ability of the player and his opponent to control them the issue of a match may depend. The reason why many contests are lost after a long lead has been established is not through any conscious decline in skill but because the will to win, anticipating that its task is over, has relaxed. The opposing will, on the other hand, has been whipped to its maximum power under the stimulus of impending defeat. The player thus challenged may think that at any time later he may regain his former ascendancy ; he will be surprised at the strength of both reactions, of his own and that of his opponent.

At these periods of disillusionment, "rubs of the court," such as net-cord strokes and doubtful line decisions, assume a mental significance beyond their true value. It almost appears as if the umpire and linesmen, elated at the turn of the tide, are leagued together to rob the player of his rightful spoils. These antagonistic phantoms will be a test of character, and the man who can meet and resist them philosophically will have a moral advantage of great value in the crisis.

CHAPTER
TEN

TACTICS IN DOUBLES

CHAPTER TEN

TACTICS IN DOUBLES

HAD lawn tennis only provided the singles game, its development as a cosmopolitan pastime, appealing to all classes, would never have been registered. For although, out of courtesy to its seniority, the singles game has always taken pride of place in the hierarchy of lawn tennis, its popular appeal has been mainly due to the adaptability of the court and its dimensions to the larger field.

Owners of private lawns in Victorian days, who were the real founders of the lawn tennis cult, would never have uprooted their croquet hoops and, in some cases, their elms, if the new pastime had not permitted successive quartettes, preferably divided in sex, to exercise themselves in friendly competition. These garden-party " fours," strong in their social appeal, were the bulwark of the game at that period ; and the principle of mixed doubles which they established was to prove the *raison d'être* of many clubs, first in England and Ireland and afterwards in progressive numbers throughout the world. Before croquet arrived, the pastimes of England had been masculine games ; it had never been the custom of women to share in them. Croquet permitted women to compete virtually on level terms with members of the other sex ; it was not to be expected that they would renounce this new experience when its successor was installed. Thus the path of the newcomer was smoothed ; and by doubles alone was its progress as a social medium assured.

Despite this claim to historical recognition, the art and science of the doubles game have never received the same measure of attention as that bestowed on the singles game. No doubt the higher prestige of the singles champion has encouraged this neglect. Another factor has been the tendency of professional instructors to teach strokes rather than tactics, to concentrate the minds of their pupils on fencing with a single-handed opposition. Then, too, the wide and heterogeneous character of tournament play has provoked scratch partnerships and the alliance of players who may either be incompatible or, because of their fugitive combination, have had no opportunity to blend their individual qualities. Considering the number of fine individual players the world has provided, it is remarkable how rarely two of them have joined forces to constitute a really great combination.

In general, the evolution of doubles play has been influenced by the same tendencies which have affected the progress of singles play. Improvement in equipment and the stimulating incentive of constant competition have quickened and intensified the pace of the rallies; the higher bound of the ball which non-turf courts provide have encouraged the freer use of the shoulder-high volley and given an added value to the half-volley; the tendency to adopt a forward base for the service return and to make that stroke the preliminary to an advancing movement towards the net has shortened the swing of the racket and invested the volleying art with greater enterprise and sparkle; the same tendency has given the lob more scope and its reply a wider range. Yet, if modern rallies are conducted at a sharper pace and with a swifter footwork than they were a couple of decades earlier, it may be doubted whether the actual quality of the strokes have been maintained, and it is certain that less attention has been paid to scientific tactics. The courts have become strewn with young and acrobatic volleyers of both sexes; very few of these pairs could survive a strategic test against masters of the doubles art.

The student of the doubles game would do well to remember that for the individual the battle-ground, in relation to the singles game, is materially reduced. The player will not only have less time and less room for swinging his racket either before or after making the stroke: in the narrower field he will be moving in a different orbit. Moreover, his changing position will depend as much on the actions of his partner as on those of his opponents; he will not be free, as in singles, to conduct the game with a single-minded purpose. The psychological reaction as well as the system of play will, therefore, be different; the test of character in doubles is even more searching than that in singles.

Doubles Pairs.

There are two kinds of effective doubles pairs. The first is a union of two players so similar in strokes and mentality that they blend, like the Doherty brothers, with a natural cohesion, forming, as it were, the double edition of one man. Since their strategic ideas are conceived in the same mould the design of one partner is automatically registered in the mind of the other ; it is as if both were playing the stroke and waiting for a result already anticipated. The advantage of this unity of purpose is obvious. If a man's confidence in his partner is such that he feels that he could not himself have played a better stroke nor made a wiser move, he is in a happy position. On the other hand, if his partner's strokes or tactics are irreconcilable with his own ideas, he will know instinctively that the cause of his side must suffer.

The other kind of team, which cannot be as strong as the first, but which has often proved its best alternative, is an alliance between two players of independent virtues so welded together by constant championship in the same court that the essence of each can be used at the proper time in a common cause. More than one combination of this character has triumphed at Wimbledon. Their unorthodox formation, paradoxical as it may seem, has been their chief strength ; for their methods, although technically unsound and, therefore, open to exposure by a team of the first category, are based on complete harmony and a perfect understanding. They may not be two men operating from the same base, but they are still two men operating with one mind ; and since their co-operation is blessed with mutual confidence and faith, they may go a long way.

Stroke values in doubles are higher than stroke values in singles. In the latter a weak stroke may be redeemed and the point saved ; in doubles the chance of a " second life " is infinitely smaller. In singles the soft answer, carefully controlled, will sometimes prove the best answer to wrath ; in doubles the soft answer is calculated to excite vengeance. The average length of a rally or rest in modern doubles, pursued by players of normal strength evenly balanced, is not more than four strokes ; it is often less in games where the service is of a destructive character. When every stroke is of intrinsic value it follows that the demand for all-round and consistent efficiency is high.

For this reason doubles are of great educational advantage to the young and inquiring player, for they reveal more rapidly than singles the virtues of positional play; they demand a greater variety of stroke; the mind must be as active as the body.

The Service.

The relation of the service to the doubles game has often been discussed. The wise captain, on winning the toss, will elect to serve, for the attack *à outrance* confers an obvious advantage. A game in hand is always worth two in prospect, and provided no accident occurs the choice of service is to be recommended. When evenly-balanced teams are opposed, the chances in favour of the serving side winning the game are about six to four. Nevertheless, the side which opens the service and retains its lead of one game cannot win the set until the service of the opposing side has been "broken through." When is that breach, essential to victory, most likely to occur? There may be something to be said for the theory that the first game of all in the set offers the best opportunity for this coup. The server may not find his range immediately; double faults in the first game are not unknown; the moral advantage of an initial "break" would undoubtedly be valuable. As against this theory must be set the fact that the receiving side will have elected to play the first game in the worse court—that is, against the sun or wind, if either or both have to be considered. The serving team will, therefore, have a double advantage. Nor is there any reason to expect that the receivers in the opening game, facing an attack with which they may not be familiar, will suddenly come to the summit of their form. More matches have been lost than won by renouncing a benefit which the spin of a racket or a coin has conferred.

Direction of Service.

The direction of the service is of primary importance in doubles play. It should be selected with two definite objects in view—the first to embarrass the receiver as much as possible (for example, by aiming at his weaker wing), and the second to force a reply which provides a decisive reprisal. For both purposes the centre line is to be recommended, not necessarily as a fixed target, but as a mark offering the best scope for sustained attack. Especially effective is it when serving from the right-hand court.

The receiver cannot often pass the server's partner down his side-line; he will be required to make a return either down the centre or across the court. In the former case his stroke will have to be very accurate and low to escape the volleyer already entrenched at the net; in the latter case he will need even more precision to outflank the advancing server. Aiming from the left-hand court down the middle line, the server may still be able to force a "volleyable" reply; the forehand diagonal return across the server's partner will not be easier than the backhand diagonal reply. Of course, the server will not so stereotype the path of his delivery that the receiver will always know what is coming. The governing rule in doubles, as in singles, is to move the receiver from his base. The server will train his guns accordingly. If, by repeatedly aiming down the middle line, he has drawn the receiver to the middle of the court, he can then select his opportunity to launch a ball near the outside line. This sudden change of direction will often win a point outright.

Variation of pace is just as essential in the server's creed as variation of direction. The ideal server is the player who surprises the receiver into making a weak stroke—one that either he or his partner can punish. It is better to deliver a medium-pace, low-bounding ball of discerning direction than a fast, high-bounding ball aimed indiscriminately. For pace begets pace. The higher the bound of the service ball the more certain is it that the receiver will essay the downward and, therefore, the least desirable reply. A low ball demands a lofted return; and since doubles play is based on manœuvring for position at the net—that is, for the pedestal position from which the ball can be hit down—the rising stroke from the opponent must be the objective. If the reckless first service is a fault and the second a soft, rising ball, the server has much the worst of the bargain; he has spent energy unnecessarily and he has offered the attack to the adversary. A controlled, well-pitched service in doubles is a great asset to the side.

The "Both up" Formation.

Since the mission of intelligent doubles play is to hit the ball down so that the opposing side may be forced to hit it up, it is essential that both players should reach the net at the earliest possible moment in pursuit of their common object, which is to end the rally with a decisive blow. The server's partner is already up; the quicker the server can gain the net position after he has launched the ball the better for his side. At all costs the latter must have crossed the service line; for if he tarries in his forward approach he will be trapped in a fatal zone and will have yielded up the advantage which the service confers. His own court rather than his partner's will be the probable objective of the receiver's return; he must regard it as a miniature singles court, offering the same positional liabilities; he must not linger in "No Man's Land"—the section between the baseline and the service-line.

"Both up" is an axiomated precept of modern doubles. In loyalty to it the partner of the receiver may be advised, like the partner of the server, to take up his position at the net. It is true that if the return of the service be weak the arrangement may have fatal consequences; for a full-blooded volley aimed direct at or through the receiver's partner will probably score outright, whereas the same stroke placed in the same direction, with the receiver's partner at the back of the court, may be retrieved and the point ultimately saved. Yet the penalty of any weak shot should be in theory fatal. If the receiver's ally be an alert and capable volleyer, his potentiality for achieving a decisive coup will be increased materially by his advanced station. The nimbler French and American volleyers have illustrated the value of this formation without dispute. It is the pedestal creed in practice. For if the receiver can dip his return to the feet of the server as he is advancing, the latter must make an upward volley. Unless this stroke be played with supreme skill the receiver's partner will be in a position to dart across the centre and make a winning retort. It is assumed, of course, that a fast and resolute match is in progress. If the receiver is weak on one wing and can only attempt a defensive reply in that region, the formation should be changed. In that case the receiver's partner may stand back for the first service and go forward for the less threatening second.

The Lob in Doubles.

The lob is a familiar stroke in the doubles game, and as a sheltering friend in bad weather—even as a match-winning expedient under certain conditions—its value cannot be denied. Yet it is essentially a signal of distress;

it advertises a disparity of stroke equipment ; the really great doubles player will only use it as a surprise variant to a frontal attack. The young player who is anxious to join the elect may be warned against its excessive cultivation ; it will tend to decrease the pace of his normal drive. One has seen a powerful doubles team undermined and finally routed by a persistent campaign of shrewd lobbing, but the victims have generally been to blame by their own tactical errors or by revealing a weakness incidental to the day. There were no two finer lobbers in the world than Beals Wright and Holcombe Ward, and these two hoisted their tosses with deadly skill against the Doherty brothers. It was the orthodox methods of the Englishmen, their all-court equipment, which won the match. When the Kinsey brothers, another American pair, beat G. L. Patterson and P. O'Hara Wood, of Australia, in the final round of the American doubles championship, it was a triumph for the lob ; yet nobody who saw this match would declare that the Kinseys were the better team nor that their methods would have prevailed against two men whose ground shots were capable of creating openings for their own volleys.

That the lob has its legitimate uses it is unnecessary to add. It can be, when thrown up suddenly, a profitable reply to the service, especially if the server is moving in at maximum speed ; but the lob must be pitched with deadly accuracy. The short lob will receive and deserve punishment, the long one may just cross the line. The function of the lob cannot be that of the drive. It is valuable for restoring a position temporarily lost or for throwing back the too eager volleyer ; strategically it must have its limitations.

Little need be added about mixed doubles. The more they are played like men's doubles, the greater is their fascination and their scope for finesse. Since youth and agility are so often their modern attributes, this department of the game has advanced markedly in quality, and a still further development may be confidently expected.

[illegible] possible [illegible] the really great doubles player will [illegible] surprise variant to a [illegible] attack. [illegible]

[illegible] the doubles, [illegible] the Doherty brothers [illegible] methods of the English [illegible] and P. [illegible] the first round [illegible] would [illegible]

[illegible]

[illegible]

CHAPTER
ELEVEN

MATCH PLAY AND PSYCHOLOGY

CHAPTER ELEVEN

MATCH PLAY AND PSYCHOLOGY

LAWN tennis matches deserving the epithet of "famous" are few and far between. Posterity has a choice and exclusive taste and will reject many of the contests upon which contemporary opinion has bestowed distinction. The historian must therefore make selection a somewhat arbitrary affair, conscious that he may have omitted from review matches that other people have deemed celebrated. In this chapter, admittedly of a rambling character, it is proposed to glance back at a few memorable engagements in the hope, likely to be fulfilled, that they will afford food for reflection both on the strategic art and on that mental attribute of every stern and challenging struggle which is called *morale*.

The exact relation of stroke quality to victory has often been debated. Purity of style is an attractive asset, and its ability to prevent physical strain and thereby conserve stamina is undeniable. But strokes of the rarest beauty cannot prevail unless the mind directing them is alive to the strategic problems which the match must present and is ready to counter the moves of an adversary who, although he may lack stroke elegance, has yet a well-trained instinct for disturbing the equanimity of those whom he encounters. Many a stylist has been broken on the wheel of match play because he has inwardly revolted against the ungainly strokes of his opponent ; the mental disturbance thus created has unsteadied his own aim.

When Jean Borotra defeated W. M. Johnston and Vincent Richards on successive days in the American championship, it was suggested in New York that both the losers had been influenced by the demeanour of the volatile Basque. When they judged him to be physically exhausted and their own campaign had cooled in consequence, he would suddenly spring into fierce action, launching a volleying attack that caught his enemies off their guard. More probably both the Americans were surprised into mistakes by the clever tactics of the Frenchman. He was not feigning fatigue as they and others imagined; he was merely parcelling out his physical reserves adroitly for a challenging test on an oppressively hot day in New York. By playing from the back of the court for two or three games in sequence he was able to practise forcing shots that, when they were followed to the net in vital games which followed, had a much keener edge and a deadlier accuracy. Maximum pressure was applied at periods which had not been signalled. This was, of course, a perfectly legitimate ruse. Of more subtle influence in both matches was the additional weight bestowed on the balls by the hour at which the contests were decided. They were able to collect the evening dew and thus to lose some of the speed which would have been their attribute early in the day. The American ball at that late hour became more like the British ball; it was a ball which an alert volleyer, to whom seconds of time were priceless for position, naturally preferred. When he met Lacoste in the final the hour was earlier, and Borotra did not get this material advantage.

No player in my fairly long experience of international lawn tennis in two hemispheres has illustrated more aptly than Borotra the art of fine generalship. The student of advanced strategy, in which the personal equation must necessarily play an important part, may profitably be directed to some of his other matches. There was his semi-final match at Wimbledon against Lacoste [1926] when, by adapting his play to meet the distinctive methods of his opponent, and by thinking in terms of "vital games," he won a notable victory. Let the loser tell the story in his own words:

"Right at the beginning of the match he noticed that I could not pass him with the aid of my backhand stroke. Instead of ceaselessly attacking my backhand stroke, which would perhaps have allowed me to tune it up, he saw the wisdom of rarely playing in the left corner of the court, contenting himself with winning his service up to four games all. But then, on four rapid returns placed on my backhand, followed by four volleys, he won my service game and the set with the following game. The second set was a repetition of the first set. During the third and fourth sets he remained at the back of the court, resting, playing on my forehand stroke, lulling me into a sense of absolute confidence. In the fifth set, however, encouraged by the public, who delighted to see him again bounding at the net after having thought him to be dying during two sets, Borotra let loose such a series of attacks on my backhand play that I could only win two games. I was filled with admiration for his intelligence and his cleverness."

Lawn tennis is a game of sequential movement, not only by the human body in producing the stroke, but in the evolution of a rally towards its decisive end. The successful player will therefore need a concentration of mind as fixed as that required for chess and other pastimes which are based on connecting moves. Literally speaking, he must lose himself in the court, conscious only of its boundaries and the flight of the ball inside them.

The best way to be crowd-proof is to develop a state of mind which is oblivious of the presence of spectators or to the proximity of any other diverting incident. A perfect illustration of the value of this attribute occurred at Forest Hills, near New York, in 1921, when Mrs. Mallory met Mlle Lenglen in the American championship. The French invader was playing her first match in a foreign environment and before a strange and curious crowd. She was obviously conscious of the conditions and affected by them. Her opponent ignored them completely. Her mind was so absorbed by the task that, when crossing over to exchange courts, she did not even recognise personal friends, and inquired of an umpire after the match whether he had been present on the day. The result was a dramatic coup by Mrs. Mallory, who won the first set with the loss of only two games and who would, no doubt, have won the second as well if Mlle Lenglen had not retired. Yet whenever these two met later, the French girl gave unquestioned proof of her superiority.

Other instances of concentrated endeavour may be given. René Lacoste mentions [*Lacoste on Tennis*] that when playing once on the centre court at Wimbledon he noticed, when serving, that his opponent had turned his back and was standing motionless on the court. Lifting his eyes, he then discovered that fifteen thousand people had risen in their seats, the King having entered the committee box. This mental detachment also served M. Lacoste in the French championship, when intermittent showers caused spectators to open and shut their umbrellas in the stand during critical rallies. His opponent was visibly disturbed by these extraneous incidents; Lacoste did not even know that rain was falling. Let the reader realise that Lacoste had trained his mind to preserve its equanimity; there was nothing cold-blooded in his nature.

Perhaps the most amazing example of concentration was that witnessed at the Craigside covered courts, Llandudno. An Indian international was due to play a singles handicap match. His powers of oblivion to the outside world were famous, but to test them decisively a wag conceived the idea of covering the faces of the ball-boys with egregious masks. This departure from normal procedure entirely escaped the notice of the immobile Indian, and he won, as he certainly deserved, a fine victory.

It will generally be found—and the moral is worth attention—that those players who have trained themselves to disregard untoward events which may occur outside the court are also unaffected by disagreeable or disturbing incidents on the court itself. The Doherty brothers were never visibly upset by an umpiring error, however patent; and it cannot be doubted that the air of unruffled serenity which characterised their play had the double result of making them strong at the moment of crisis and of conserving their energy over a long match. Their mind was never tormented by a retrospect so often fatal to the task in hand. Victims of an umpiring lapse may be advised to remember that what really matters is not the loss of a single point, but the loss of control which any exhibition of annoyance at the incident betrays.

I have already mentioned one famous ladies' match; in the same category of distinction may be placed two others in which Mlle Lenglen figured. The first opened her incomparable career at Wimbledon; the second, seven years later, virtually ended her amateur triumphs in France. In 1919 there came to the centre court for the first time a young girl who, taught as a child by her father, had developed her skill by practice with men in the South of France. At the age of fifteen she had won the hard-court championship of the world at St. Cloud; but the War intervened and the prodigy of 1914 had enjoyed no previous experience of a turf surface. Her game in 1919 was not then the art, perfect in poise and restrained power, which it since became, but it was a game founded on the fundamentals of the masters; its ground-stroke accuracy was phenomenal and it possessed a variety of strokes which strained no department to the detriment of another. Meeting Mrs. Larcombe in the second round, the invader emerged from this test with flying colours ; subtle finesse did not alarm her, and she only lost three games. Mrs. Craddock and Miss McKane gave her no trouble ; Miss Ryan's menacing chops were beaten off in two sets, though each was close. An easy victory over Mrs. Satterthwaite brought "Suzanne" to Mrs. Lambert Chambers.

This match, absorbing a crowd of eight thousand, headed by the King and Queen and Princess Mary, was, without question, the finest ladies' singles ever seen at Wimbledon. Whatever the score might be, the international character of the duel, the contrasting personalities and ages of the rivals, and the fact that France, through its girl champion, was laying siege to a British stronghold, must have held public interest. But the play itself was worthy of the occasion, its vicissitudes remarkable, and its finish a wonderful climax. The holder was certainly not the favourite before the event ; the smooth progress of the challenger through the All-Comers was an augury of her success. Yet Mrs. Lambert Chambers, accurate in all her strokes, consistently resolute in attack and vigilant in defence, amazingly mobile on a very hot day, was twice within a stroke of victory. She allowed Mlle Lenglen, it is true, to rob her of a lead in the first set of eighteen games, but in the early stages the French girl had scarcely come to her zenith. Allowing no thought of the past to depress her, Mrs. Chambers took the second set at 6–4, an equally close struggle, though eight games less were waged in it. The prospect of a third set seemed at first to unnerve the exhausted challenger. She questioned her own physical powers and rested at the foot of the umpire's chair for a period rather beyond the normal. Her opponent stood waiting, then took a linesman's chair kindly vacated. A lump of sugar, tinctured with cognac, was cast on to the court by M. Lenglen from his seat in the stand.

Thus fortified, his daughter renewed the combat and to such good purpose that she went forward to 4–1, apparently a commanding lead. Mrs. Chambers now fought heroically for her country and her championship. Pressing her strongest claims at the stage of the French reaction, she squared the match and pressed on, in an electric atmosphere, every stroke riveting attention, to lead 6–5 and 40–15. The young challenger, the prize seemingly about to slip from her grasp, faced this ordeal with exemplary courage. She neither flinched nor faltered, but she enjoyed the fortune of the brave. Mrs. Chambers saw her opening and took it ; in desperation Mlle Lenglen, from a losing position near the middle of the court, put her racket in the way of a winning drive. The ball struck the gut near the wooden frame and recrossed the net—to the surprise and momentary paralysis of the champion. Had she expected this lucky reply Mrs. Chambers might yet have won the point and preserved the title. The reprieved challenger went on to win the match. Her next shot, making the score deuce, was a beautiful backhand drive down the line, which raised chalk. She was never again within a stroke of defeat, although tension and fine tennis were maintained to the very end. Viewed from any angle the struggle was memorable. The percentage of stroke error by both players was almost negligible ; the net was rarely shaken by a mistimed drive. One incident illustrating its hectic close may be recorded—the planting of a kiss on the winner's cheek by Max Decugis, the first Frenchman to win a tournament in England.

Her match against Miss Helen Wills on the Carlton courts at Cannes in 1926 was probably a greater ordeal for Mlle Lenglen. It was memorable for the world-wide publicity which it attracted, for the tactical acumen of the French player, and for an exhibition of remarkable tenacity under severe mental strain on the part of both competitors. Mlle Lenglen's fluent footwork and skilful placing were never better illustrated. Had she fed Miss Wills, as she might have fed other antagonists, with deep-length drives she might have found the vigour of the American attack off the ground too strong ; instead, by a delicate variation of speed, she drew Miss Wills forward, so that she was required to make many of her shots from a relatively slow ball and, when running forward, she was unable to employ the shoulder rotation which is a feature of her robust driving. When she was within a stroke of the match in the long second set, a member of the excited gallery, anticipating the end, exclaimed " Out " when Miss Wills made a fine forehand drive down the line. Both players deemed the match over ; a wild throng burst on to the court. But the linesman had not spoken. When he made this fact clear to the umpire, the threads of a feverish struggle, with both players well-nigh exhausted, had to be picked up again. Mlle Lenglen lost the critical game and also its successor ; that she regained the ascendency and finally won the essential points for victory, in spite of a moral reaction which must have been almost unprecedented, was an enduring example of will-power. One may regard this match and the courageous resistance exhibited by the French and American champions as finally and utterly destroying the legend that women of forceful character cannot face a psychological crisis in sport with the same composure as men.

It is a mistake to suppose—and lesser lights may take comfort from the fact—that great players do not conceal behind their apparent confidence and fluency of stroke the normal emotions of mankind. It is no superhuman quality but a philosophy born of experience which helps them to preserve the spirit of outward calm. The inscrutable demeanour worn by Norman Brookes during his big matches was a valuable asset, since it communicated an impression of iron resolve to his opponents. Off the court the famous Australian was not in the least awe-inspiring ; on court he seemed to exercise through his personality a kind of moral suasion over the minds of his opponents. Probably the feeling of impotency was engendered by the style of the Australian. He was left-handed, and thus, at the old Wimbledon at any rate, was not harassed nearly as much by the sun when he served from the sunny side. He played his backhand volleys with the same side of the racket as for the forehand, and by bending the head down struck many of the lofted balls at the level of the eyes, thus improving his marksmanship. It is sometimes possible to anticipate the direction of an opponent's shot by " reading the eyes." Those of Norman Brookes were concealed from view by a cloth cap. Thus he was provided with accessories which aided and abetted his court-craft. Perhaps he was conscious of the fact and exploited it legitimately to his advantage.

Lawn tennis is not credited with the team virtues of older games, yet the isolation of the player in singles has its advantage in the development of character, since it demands and will train self-reliance and quick decision. Mlle Lenglen and René Lacoste were shy and nervous children ; match play in public proved an unrivalled tonic. In no other public pastime is the gaze of a crowd so close and so continuous. This concentration of spectators imposes a concentration on the player ; it ought to develop the best that is in him ; and if the worst should by chance come out, he will know that it is condemned by public opinion.

But lawn tennis is not wholly or exclusively a game for the expression of individualism. Team matches have multiplied in every country ; the junior of both sexes has an ever-increasing opportunity to play for his side. Here judicious and sympathetic captaincy has its scope ; here the value of collective progress is advertised. The rise of national or sectional supremacy may be traced directly to the personal influence of great players reacting through those in their immediate company. Certain countries and certain clubs have risen to eminence, overcoming all resistance, because a group of players have pooled and exchanged their tactical knowledge, not reserving it for selfish use in tournament play. On the other hand, countries and clubs have suffered, and the game with it, because the gulf between the players and the executive has been too wide for effective liaison. Davis Cup matches have been lost because the team has been selected by men not themselves cognisant with the conditions of an era which they have left behind and who are thus unable to communicate their faith to or inspire those whom they choose.

CHAPTER TWELVE

SOME REFLECTIONS ON TRAINING

CHAPTER TWELVE

SOME REFLECTIONS ON TRAINING

AN origin almost fortuitous, casual rather than organised development, and an interest which is utilitarian rather than scientific, have created a popular impression that lawn tennis can be pursued without physical training. The detachment may be accepted if nothing more serious or strenuous is contemplated than a light-hearted " knock-up " on a neighbour's court. Yet even the neophyte will discover that his attraction for the game will increase in direct ratio to his ability, by moving quickly over the court, to keep in contact with the ball. Mobility is supposed to be the prerogative of youth ; but a man is as old as he runs. The fact that many players over thirty years of age, and some, indeed, over forty, not only move as rapidly on court as players under thirty, but appear to contain their energy over a longer period, suggests that experience has provided them with practical expedients for preserving stamina.

The social attributes of lawn tennis, it must be admitted, are not conduciveto spartan training. With rare exceptions the game has not been admitted to the curriculum of Public Schools in Great Britain, although its recognition in America on that basis is universal, and it is encouraged freely as a school game in other countries. One result of its exclusion from school sports in the land which founded lawn tennis and contains Wimbledon is the tendency of youth to pursue it in later years without due regard to physical requirements or moral obligations. The traditions of fitness have not been planted ; the boy has rarely been encouraged to go " all out " at a game which, if it is to be mastered and fully enjoyed, demands as much physical exertion, and will bestow as much benefit on health, as games that are more honoured.

One may ask whether, if the mentors of youth had appreciated, like the competitors themselves, the stress and strain of a championship fortnight at Wimbledon,

England would have been excluded from the singles title-rôle for over twenty years?

For what does a hard singles match of five sets involve? The physical effort may be continuous and exacting for over two hours. It does not consist only of traversing up and down and across the court and swinging a racket as one might swing a cane in a field of daisies; the whole body and sometimes the whole weight of the body must be used in the execution of strokes. It is a case of creating power and controlling power all the time, and of so grading its distribution that reserves are held back for an emergency the exact advent of which in a close engagement can never be timed. The idea that such an ordeal (which J. C. Parke, an international player at both games, claimed was more severe than a Rugby football match) does not require careful and assiduous preparation and can be adequately sustained without it is, of course, to reject every athletic experience. Against the rare instances where men have won important contests in spite of a neglect of training, there are many where the "fit man" of inferior stroke skill has defeated the player more brilliant but less careful in training than himself. Anthony Wilding, Zenzo Shimizu, and J. C. Parke may be mentioned in this connection. These players could always be relied upon to stay the course, however hard the going.

On the general question of bodily fitness in relation to arduous match play I cannot do better than summarise some observations offered by a well-known medical man whose practice brought him into daily contact with athletes. He was insistent that the much-talked of "condition" should not be a specialism but a rule of life; that there was no such thing as a quick cure for ills and weaknesses which habit had created. Here are some of his wise remarks [*Complete Lawn Tennis Player* (Methuen)]:

"To compass a great task which never must be a great strain, all muscles must be gradually prepared, and the heart is a muscle. To make preparation and performance easy, what suits the stomach, as easy of digestion, suits the preparation for the task, and the stomach is a tyrant. In mechanical engines free lubrication and the avoidance of heated bearings go together as precautionary measures for easy working. The lungs are the body's engine and the lungs want all possible attention. Their carbon or fuel comes from the blood, therefore the blood must contain fuel-elements, and the heart as the stoker 'slumbers not nor sleeps.'

"You need, then, blood-food put into the blood which it can distribute to the muscles and the lungs as the middleman of supply and distribution; the wholesale agent is the stomach, the retailers the other organs concerned in digestion. The dustman or waste-remover is needed; and this is shared by the excretory organs. As the highest culture involves a sense of proportion so the higher bodily efficacy involves the perfection of balance—balance as to supply and waste. The riddle is (and a very soluble one it is) how to adjust food, select food, supply food—distribution is the blood's work—and then how to help the skin, secure the due and proper action of the bowels, and assist the kidneys to perform their functions. The blood distributes the materials for nutrition. We have to regulate our lives that these materials are properly used. The equipoise is 'condition.'

"The aesthetics of food are over when we have swallowed. Believe me that very accurate and discrimating chemist, the blood, despises vintages, thinks very little of high living, and altogether disowns luxury as a *sine qua non.* The blood has elementary and fundamental first principles and to first principles he reduces all that is sent him by the stomach to 'sample.' His labelling is extremely simple. He will find his vital element in the most ordinary diet. You may tickle your palate with all sorts of expensive things and yet your value to him is only as to how far he can find in them his vital elements when all the organs concerned in digestion have retailed their residues. He wastes nothing of value; you do that beforehand, and he is out of that wasteful competition. What shall you send to that wholesaler, the stomach, to distribute to the retail shops—the other organs concerned in digestion? That is the puzzle. The perpetual customer is the blood. He wants all from them that is of value to him: what is valueless he says 'No, thank you' to. And the retail shops only receive what they are ordained to 'handle.' There is no waste in Nature: waste is man's patent.

"To compass condition the teeth, eyes, ears, and breathing apparatus must be known to be in good order. Rotten teeth, mal-adjusted vision, wax-loaded ears, and nasal defects which render proper breathing impossible all need primary, and never perfunctory attention. So, too, the hygiene of our houses must be good and especially the air-supply of our bedrooms.

"I say nothing of the food a well-to-do or wealthy amateur may take for the purpose of training, for I am more concerned to make 'condition' within the food-reach of all. And so I will only note what I consider necessary and within the power of any man's pocket to obtain. Tea, bread, butter, ham, fresh meat, potatoes, cabbage, cheese. There are the necessaries. These can be varied with porridge, milk, oatmeal, broth, meat, green food, bread and butter, and the changes rung between the two. In the British climate it is not every man who could train on a vegetable diet, but it is done and can be done. It must be remembered that climate has its own claims to notice. Train in Northumberland or Norfolk and then suddenly and without climatic preparation try and play in Cannes or California, and it would mean a very unusual man to be at his best in such sudden transition.

"For great tasks and a set ordeal of any kind (lawn tennis included) the law is uniform. There may be variations as to specific muscle-training, and, no doubt, the walker and the lawn tennis player would go on to special and divergent loop-lines at a point of their training. But the law of the body is inexorably the same as to the main issues of demand on rules of health. For most men preparing for ordeals of a severe kind alcohol is unnecessary, smoking is unwise, and early hours are essential—early at each end of the day I mean. I have a great addiction to the recommending of fencing as an adjunct for all training. I know no other exercise which so trains nerve, eye, and muscle and no similar pastime for keeping the skin supple and in perfect order. I have every belief in Sandow exercises for arm-suppleness and the increasing of reach, and I do not think I could speak too highly of the properly managed Turkish bath."

Since this advice was tendered the nervous and physical strain of championship lawn tennis, due to its wider international vogue, its fiercer competition, and the piercing light of publicity shed on its champions, has increased; the need for self-denial and disciplined training has correspondingly been strengthened. Those who have acknowledged this truth have done best. Lacoste became a living example of what rigorous training can achieve, for he was a delicate and fragile child and only developed his powers of endurance by a practical regime carefully considered and as carefully maintained. He had great faith in breathing exercises in the open air, but when he was competing in a tournament he shortened their duration, conscious that too much detailed preparation on the day of a match was a psychological error. Similarly he had less skipping exercises in the morning during a tournament. He believed in the comforting serenity of habits, tested for their wholesome benefit ; to remember in the crisis of a match that there has been no previous abuse inspires confidence. Lacoste mentions an occasion at Wimbledon when he lunched later than usual before an important match. " I played well in the first set," he recalled, " but during the entire second set I could not play for lack of breath. It was only at the end of the third set that I could resume my normal game."

On the question of food, W. O'Brien, the American Davis Cup trainer, held the view that too much playing and too much eating were the surest means of incurring unexpected defeat. He advised [*American Lawn Tennis*] players, during a tournament, to limit themselves to two meals a day, breakfast and dinner. If there was a feeling of hunger in the middle of the day he suggested that a baked apple and tea and toast were ample to satisfy it ; even this repast should be taken two hours before play.

One may note that Tilden never touched alcohol during his championship career. He was a moderate smoker, but cut it out entirely during his earlier Davis Cup tours. " I found it injured my wind and slowed up my focusing powers materially," he wrote. On the vexed question of staleness Mr. Tilden's view is worth quoting. " Staleness," he wrote [*Singles and Doubles*], " is not a question of playing too much tennis, for staleness is a mental condition expressed in terms of a physical reaction." To combat it the game must be moderated but not necessarily suspended altogether. Tilden's own preference is for the cinema and bridge. During his Australian tour he rented a gramophone and reproduced the voices of Caruso, Melba, and May Garden. But he was careful to eschew the moving picture on the night before a big match.

Various methods have been practised for restoring " tone " after an arduous match. The player of good health and moderate habits will respond to Nature's normal remedies, but he will be wise to regard alcohol as a traitorous friend. Any large dose of liquid refreshment, including soft, iced drinks, freely offered in America, has the danger of suddenly changing the temperature of the body and thus hindering the ordinary recuperative agencies. When certain muscles have been strained severely, it will be found that the moderate use of other muscles has beneficial and often immediate results. When M. Borotra, seemingly on the threshold of a physical collapse, had finished a strenuous international match at Philadelphia, the dressing-room attendant, an old college trainer, urged him to take exercise in a swimming bath. He accepted the hint and with such good results that he was able to wage another hard match on the same day.

Mr. J. Parmly Paret, the American authority, suggests other rapid remedies which have their value. "When a man is badly exhausted," he writes [*American Sportsman's Library*], "an excellent method of reviving him is to use a stiff brush for rubbing the skin, particularly over the muscles which are most used, after it has been thoroughly dried of all perspiration. After rubbing with a brush until the skin turns pink, a short application of clear alcohol and some massage of the muscles will revive an exhausted man very quickly. When a tennis match is finally over, the player should lie down and rest for at least ten or fifteen minutes, in order that the blood may cool and the flow of perspiration stop, before taking the usual shower-bath or dressing. To check the perspiration too quickly is injurious, and if he takes his bath or dresses before the blood has cooled off, it will break out again immediately after. One other suggestion I can offer, that has proved very useful to me and may be welcomed by other players of a nervous temperament. If one feels anxious about the results of an important match, one's nerves are very likely to be unsteady, and if this nervousness appears in the stomach, as it frequently has with me, a splendid way to stop it is to eat half a cracker or a small morsel of dry bread just before going on the court. The fresh food will not be enough to interfere with one's activity and the nervousness will soon disappear."

Cramp in varying degree—sometimes so severe as to "knock-out" a player—is associated with lawn tennis matches. Dr. A. A. Warden, of Cannes, a well-known player of proved stamina, believes that in many cases the attack is due to the fact that the muscles have been starved of their normal supply in the blood of sodium chloride.

He suggests that sufferers from this complaint should take at the beginning of each set a tablet of a few grains—10 to 15—of common salt with a little water, and continue to swallow small sips to keep away extreme thirst and dryness of the lips.

This theory is confirmed by scientific investigation carried out in the experimental chamber of the Mining Research Laboratory at the University of Birmingham. Acute attacks of cramp were well known to occur among miners and others engaged in hard work in hot places when water was freely consumed. According to Mr. W. Hancock, Ph.D., hard muscular labour and the drinking of water to quench thirst were the two conditions which appear to determine such attacks. " It was clear," says this authority [*British Medical Journal*], " that if a man was perspiring freely, and at the same time replacing the lost fluid by drinking water, there would be a tendency for the percentage of chloride in the blood plasma and in the whole body to fall (since much chloride might be lost in the sweat), with a corresponding tendency to a fall in the osmotic pressure of the blood plasma. In the ordinary way this tendency was countered by the action of the kidneys, which excreted excess of water while retaining the chloride ; but during hard muscular work the kidneys were thrown almost out of action owing to the division of blood supply to the muscles, whereupon the body was left defenceless against the effects of loss of chloride. In addition to this violent and painful cramp, a group of milder symptoms might result, such as depression and fatigue, when the supply of sodium chloride to the body was insufficient to meet the greatly increased loss due to much sweating."

Many players might object to drinking salt water, even in sips, but salt can very easily be put up into small coated pills. Alternatives, as the Swiss guides find, are sugar or chocolate—the former, by the way, freely used by tournament players in all countries as an aid to stamina.

Earlier in this volume, in discussing stroke production, the virtue of style in relation to endurance was emphasised. In this connection it is significant that players with the most fluent strokes, produced without apparent effort, rarely, if ever, suffered from cramp. One may instance in particular, H. L. Doherty, Mlle Lenglen, H. Cochet, and R. N. Williams. It is when strokes are made in a way inviting a strain on one section of the body which the other sections cannot, by their orderly co-operation, relieve, that Nature rebels. That common enemy to play, "tennis elbow," has been dividing medical opinion ever since it was first experienced. When this complaint was discussed at a meeting of the Section of Orthopædics of the Royal Society of Medicine [December 3, 1929], the chairman said he was quite prepared to disagree with nearly all the learned authorities who had spoken on the subject. The etiology of tennis elbow remained undetermined, its pathology obscure, and its cure uncertain. It is at least tenable, having regard to the methods of players who are usually its chief victims, that tennis elbow is the result of incorrect, or, at any rate, inadequate stroke play. If this is so, its cure would appear to be obvious although difficult. It is significant that the malady, as a rule, comes on so gradually that it is difficult for the patient to say exactly when the condition arose; also that it seems to yield more pain when the backhand drive, generally the stroke played with less confidence and facility, is attempted.

Various remedial measures have their supporters, such as rest, massage, a restrictive splint, the electrolyte needle, and manipulation. Dr. W. H. Trethowan, Orthopædic Surgeon to Guy's Hospital, has declared that in a series of grave cases after a clear and complete view of the joint involved, the blood having been withdrawn from the tissues, he found no abnormal condition of the surrounding muscles or ligaments. But in each case he discovered an "inflamed fringe of the lining membrane of the joint, a congested area from which it had been impossible to expel all the contained blood. By the removal of these fringes a cure was obtained in all cases." Mr. Trethowan advances the theory that tennis elbow is always an "inflammatory condition of the radio-humeral joint," the inflammation being due to slight and repeated injuries in the shape of shocks or pinchings during certain movements. In the early stages, often neglected by ardent players, rest is essential. In more prolonged cases rest may result in the inflamed tissues forming adhesions or wrinkles inside the joint. Here the skilful manipulator, by breaking these down, can produce and justly claim credit for relief of the condition.

A final word about blisters of the skin. These will naturally occur, either on foot or hand, more often at the beginning of the season. Foot blisters are often caused by the change from a stiff walking shoe with a high heel to a flexible shoe with a low heel and to the sudden use of muscles little exercised. Since these muscles are subjected to the same law as other muscles, it is only natural, after a long period of inactivity, that they should revolt. Regular physical exercise in low-heeled shoes will obviate the trouble. An efficacious remedy against blistered feet or hands, applied at the first sign of trouble, and before there is any fracture of the skin, is a mixture of whisky and salad oil painted over the tender portion. This application will harden the skin and usually "do the trick."

CHAPTER
THIRTEEN

MODERN MASTERS AND THEIR METHODS

CHAPTER THIRTEEN

MODERN MASTERS AND THEIR METHODS

I. *W. T. Tilden*

IN *Advice to His Son* the Earl of Chesterfield remarked that although he would not give one farthing for virtue he would give ten thousand pounds for a character, knowing that he would get ten thousand pounds out of it.

These brief analytical sketches will not of intent catalogue the virtues of champions. Rather are they designed for the purpose of suggesting the methods of physical and mental training which have brought these players to the front. If those methods differ, both in substance and degree, the inference is provoked deliberately that lawn tennis, being a game of individual expression, is essentially a pursuit where individual character must influence success. Men and women have commanded it in the past, and will command it in the future, not exclusively through the virtue of their stroke play. Some of them may even lack a pleasing style yet discount the defect in match play by tactical acumen or a courage more timely than a steady aim. For it is the qualities of the heart and head just as much as of the hand that in the searching test yield victory.

I begin with William T. Tilden, the American champion for seven years out of ten, not because he has always been invincible; rather because, of the careers of all great players, Tilden's emphasises, perhaps most vividly, the value of character. He came, like some of his British ancestors, of an iconoclastic stock; he was a rebel from youth. Because of this independence, this repugnance to conventional restraint, he always appealed to the younger generation. By teaching boys to play lawn tennis he taught himself; the progress of both was assisted by mutual admiration. Tilden, the self-imposed teacher, labouring not for self-interest but for mass influence, was forced to concentrate on his task in order that the pupils' faith in the power of their mentor might not be shaken.

Thus there was a conspiracy of mutual instruction ; the eager and sanguine mind of the leader gripped in practice principles which no text-book and no coach could teach.

Aggression has always been the feature of the American game. The note of defiance is struck in the first stroke ; the point is not deemed patriotically won unless the same spirit is associated with the last. There was a period before Tilden flowered when the service and the volley almost exclusively ruled the court ; but for the Dohertys these specialised methods would have prevailed at Wimbledon. The first tactical task, then, of Tilden, as of his great contemporary, W. M. Johnston, was to nullify the break service and to burke the man who followed it to the net. Both objects were obtained through the same weapon—a courageous, reliable, and deftly-controlled drive. Following R. N. Williams who, trained in Europe, had shown them the way, these two reasserted and refined the principles of sound ground strokes. But their baseline play did not come to full maturity until each pursued it against the other. Tilden did not find his pole in the American volleyers ; he found it in Williams and Johnston ; he could not have become the complete player without the complete opposition.

Tilden's service and driving power were no doubt aided by his stature and his build ; his shoulder blades had unusual height and strength ; photograph him in a group and the fact became patent. His capacity for endurance —never assisted, by the way, by an alcoholic stimulant— was above the ordinary. But these physical attributes would have been of little avail without versatility of stroke and generalship. Tilden was no ready-made champion ; he had to foster his genius by industry and control his temperament by philosophy. In his earliest tournaments he had as much trouble with his mentality as with his opponents ; even to-day he is peculiarly sensitive to environment.

Turf was his natural surface. It must be so with all players who can exploit every stroke to obtain a desired effect. The non-turf court, whether it be of burnt clay or cement, will never yield as tractably to the aggression of a full-blooded service or drive, nor respond as readily to the more subtle attention of graded speed and spin. The grass court has always been, and must remain, the plane for the fullest exercise of the game's art, and since Tilden is nothing if not a complete artist he must prefer the grass court. Both footwork and stroke timing, co-related as they are, need for Tilden, as for most men of his stature, the turf surface.

Footwork is the agency for perfect weight, control, and balance ; timing is the transfer of the player's weight into his stroke—the generator of pace. The first begets the second ; the ball of the foot is influenced as much by the resistance of the floor as the ball itself. Tilden admitted that he was not born with a sense of perfect timing ; he only acquired it by studying the laws of footwork. It was his belief that few players realise that they are almost always on the wrong foot in making a shot ; and even when their feet are right their weight may be transferred at the wrong moment. He warned the young players against looking either at the opposite side of the court or at his opponent. The dimensions of the first are static ; the movements of the second cannot be controlled. The eye's objective should always be the ball. This is axiomatic advice ; Tilden developed it into a science. You wonder why he hit the objective lines so frequently ; it was because his subjective mind had rehearsed unfalteringly the connecting passages. He gained that path blindfolded, as it were ; the way would have been blocked if his footwork had been fractionally faulty.

He uses a racket weighing $13\frac{1}{4}$ ounces. Unstrung its weight is half an ounce less. Its handle is $4\frac{7}{8}$ inches at the holding end. His grip, or hold, is changed for the forehand and backhand and also for the volley. He reverses the face of the racket for his forehand and backhand drives. For the full forehand shot the line of the arm, wrist, and racket is straight. For the backhand stroke he moves the hand counter-clockwise on the handle for a quarter of a circle. The wrist is above it, locked stiff ; there is again a straight line of arm, hand, and weapon. He does not use the thumb up the handle. His service grip, like his volleying grip, is mid-way between the forehand- and backhand-drive grip. It is also his grip for the slice or chop. The wrist, then, is always below the racket head. Without these variations in grip, Tilden would not have achieved his complete and masterly variation of stroke.

II. *H. Cochet.*

When a player, as Henri Cochet did in 1927, wins the singles title at Wimbledon after forfeiting the first two sets in his last three matches, he must be endowed with qualities denied to his fellows. His successive and beaten opponents in that year were F. T. Hunter, Tilden, and Borotra—all men of strength and courage; the cause of Cochet's triumph in each was not due to any moral collapse on their part.

Cochet did not cultivate style—that is, the art of making strokes without physical reaction, cumulative in long matches; he was endowed with it, like H. L. Doherty. Therefore, while maturing, he had no faults of technique to correct; instinctively he graduated length and strength by perfect timing; the ball obeyed his mind rather than his muscle. Thus a temperament, normally under control, was not excited or depressed, as other temperaments might be, by a realisation of some weakness in stroke structure or some limitation in power. To Cochet every stroke on the board was possible, every refinement of the game's art could be explored.

This knowledge of versatility, of an unrivalled range of stroke, gave him two supreme advantages. He was confident at the moment of peril, for he could always summon a complete equipment to his aid. His anatomy was never rebelling in the crisis of a fifth set against the strain imposed by the production of an unorthodox shot. The practice of the preceding sets had only served to polish and refine his strokes in the final set; he could be at his best, with stamina unimpaired, at the end.

Commanding every stroke of the regulation pattern, he did not need excessive speed of service or drive. Like the first great player of all, William Renshaw, who had no model to imitate, he could fix his own bases on the court. From the normally losing position he could often achieve, by dint of his instinctive skill, a winning coup. He could stand within a yard of the service line to receive the cannon-ball service of W. T. Tilden. His racket met the ball on the rise, forming as it were a resilient cushion for the swift rebound. This forward position gave him an obvious advantage as a volleyer; the advance was a synthetic movement; the opponent was almost paralysed by an attack so perfect in its balance and riposte.

This superb talent of Cochet, with force and finesse so cunningly combined, could be challenged and sometimes frustrated by the staunch ground strokes of Lacoste or an inspired counter-volleying attack from Borotra; it still preserved its inestimable virtue of style; technically his equipment must always be more efficient, more likely to prevail in the long run.

He has the defects of his qualities. Supreme, though never contemptuous, self-confidence makes him careless or casual against opponents who cannot provide a strategic problem. This is why he often loses sets and may sometimes, on less important occasions, lose matches. But he is a player endowed with a genius that is at once natural and supreme.

III. *René Lacoste.*

If Dr. Smiles had drawn his morals from sport and not from commerce he would have found in René Lacoste a living example of "Self-Help." Until he was thirteen years of age this son of France had not seen a lawn tennis court; by the time he was twenty-one he had won the championships of France, Britain, and America. Willie Renshaw was twenty when he first won the singles at Wimbledon, but R. F. Doherty did not attain the same honour until his twenty-third year, H. L. Doherty not before his twenty-sixth. Lacoste's career, indeed, is unique in the annals of the game, since the schoolboy champion of France transformed himself into the champion of two hemispheres entirely by self-discipline and an inherent determination to conquer every scientific problem that lawn tennis could offer.

If he accomplished this task in record time he also accomplished it by record industry. His zeal was no less consumable than his patience. He was punctilio personified over practice and training; no detail was too small for consideration; over no self-imposed ordinance did he weaken. Before his conquests were complete he jotted down in a little notebook every characteristic of stroke and strategy of his chief opponents; this memorandum he studied as a general would study a war chart.

Two illustrations of his assiduity and his attention to small things may be given. He had noticed at his earlier tournaments that competitors, after removing their wraps for the preliminary knock-up, had sometimes to await the arrival of the balls. Lacoste foresaw the possibility of beginning to play with chilled muscles. He made it a rule to tuck a box of balls under his arm before entering the court. Again, at Philadelphia, before meeting W. T. Tilden in the Davis Cup-tie, the ping of his racket could be heard on the eve of the match as the ball was hit to and fro against the wall of the stand—it was too dark to perceive the striker.

The same youth, when wintering in his father's house at Courboie, Paris, would use a spare room as training quarters. He needed no adversary; he did not even require a net; a bare wall sufficed. And when he was away from this "court," which had no lines, he found an adequate substitute in any piece of furniture that would accept a cushion. Into this impressionable shield he would discharge tennis balls. Their fate after they had left his racket did not concern him; he was concentrating on the production of the stroke.

Lacoste became the most efficient stroke player in the world. He mastered, and by the written word interpreted, the mechanics of the game. His style, acquired through application and not as a birthright, might be less idealistic than that of Cochet; it remained loyal to orthodoxy, unfettered in its swing, polished in its refinement. Both his forehand and backhand drives, the latter especially, were productions of perfect hip action. The arm, crooked at the elbow for the swing back, moved round from the shoulder, with the hip forming the compressionable spring; its repercussion gave the motive power for the subsequent blow. Needless to say, the feet were perfectly pivoted to give these choice results.

When he had nothing left to learn about driving, Lacoste tackled the volleying art. His improvement in this department became a feature of his later matches.

IV. *Jean Borotra*

France rose to her eminence partly by virtue of her discovery that the modern game of lawn tennis provided an æsthetic substitute for the royal and ancient game of tennis at which her countrymen excelled centuries ago, and partly because, after the long siege which the war imposed, four players emerged who could advance simultaneously, finding counsel and inspiration in each other's success. It was this illustrious group which, like other groups in other countries in the past, although more markedly, lifted France to the top of the international ladder.

Lacoste's industry and discipline, Cochet's instinctive genius, Brugnon's quiet and unobtrusive power, all played their part; but it was the energising influence of Jean Borotra and his sanguine spirit which quickened and repeated victory. His was the physical buoyancy, oozing from the Pyrenees, which initiated attack; his the resolution which faced and fenced with forces others might fear;

his the ambition which placed no definite boundary on progress. Borotra's personality, even more than his play, was the asset of France.

He started as, and remained, an unorthodox player. No coach had tutored him ; he taught the whole world a new gospel. He did not drive the ball—he had not time for the elegancies of the drive ; he lunged at it, prodded it, pushed it. Neither the feet were straddled nor the racket held according to text-book law ; strokes were frequently made with the weight on a foot which was apparently travelling out of its natural orbit. Volleys that neither E. W. Lewis nor Norman Brookes ever attempted were made from losing positions.

But if Borotra's style is unconventional—a law, indeed, to his lithesome, volatile body—the brain behind his game is of the shrewdest. He is a great match player, perhaps the greatest of his epoch. A ripe student of tactics, he is still a riper student of his opponent's methods and moods. None can read more accurately his adversary's intention, none conceal his own design more cunningly, none strike with better precision or more effect at the right moment. If the mass psychology of the crowd can spur him on, it is his talent for probing other people's psychology which wins him close matches.

Moving and turning so rapidly, always carried forward by his own momentum, the net is his natural objective—indeed his only barrier. His toe-work is so fluent and his limbs so lissom that, like a kingfisher, he can dart from point to point, bending or rising as the ball's oncoming flight might demand. Thus nothing but the perfect passing shot or the perfect lob could elude his volleyer's art, rendered much more effective because of its nimble daring.

In later years Borotra materially strengthened his ground strokes. They still defied normal canons ; because the usual swing was not behind them, their surprise value increased. Many a point was won from the court's corners by a stroke seemingly extracted from nothing except an agile spring. Borotra's backhand return of service off a rising ball became one of the most brilliant shots in international lawn tennis—to the spectator it was merely the flashlike flick of an extended arm.

His best floors are wood and turf. They minister to his mobility ; he can turn sharply on either ; both courts accept the ball-spin which he uses so freely. In a covered court, perhaps, he is seen to best advantage, not only because the surface suits his strokes and footwork but because the walls and roof stimulate that "arena" sense—or what may be called *milieu de l'occasion*—upon which a player so masterful can feed.

V. *H. W. Austin.*

England, crowning no singles champion on the male side at Wimbledon for twenty years, placed a player in the semi-final round in 1929. The feat was none too soon nor decisive, yet it was an earnest of the turning tide—perhaps "a happy prologue to the swelling act."

Better than the actual performance was the style and methods of the performer. H. W. Austin not only defeated a string of oversea invaders; he reincarnated the principles of mastery by which H. L. Doherty had held the champions of other countries at bay. The faith in the orthodoxy of British strokes was vindicated; the secret of the Doherty regime was again revealed. This was balm to many tortured souls.

Austin has not yet quite reached Doherty's class, for his Cambridge predecessor was nothing if not a complete player; he had no weakness in a finished game. Nevertheless, if his overhead play, whether in service or smash, is not comparable with that of Doherty, nor his reserves of stamina so carefully martialled, his strokes off the ground and on the low volley has as much merit; there is the same instinctive control and the same intuitive tactical skill. Moreover, since the pace and variety of attack have admittedly quickened in the last two decades, although its refinement might be less, Austin has proved his hardihood and his capacity for resistance by defeating modern gladiators.

His game, like that of Doherty, and of Lacoste and Cochet after him, is founded on correct rhythm, which means fluent and sequential movement of the body, each segment playing its part. He does not "hit" the ball over the net; rather is it "swept" to its place, as if its advent were incidental to the physical exercise. Players of this rare type—Mlle Lenglen was another example—do not employ abnormal force; their speed comes from perfect timing, which is the product of perfect balance and poise; they borrow as much pace from their opponent's strokes as they have need to generate themselves. For their rackets in many rests are but "shock-absorbers" or shields for the blows of their adversaries. By their agility of hand and foot they can employ the principle of repercussion, none too widely appreciated on the lawn tennis court.

Like Doherty, Austin is at his best on a grass court. He finds in the turf cushion the best "spring-board" for his delicate footwork and the best "clearing-house" for his low drives. The quicker Austin's shots are carried out of the opponent's reach, and the less the height of their bound, the stronger is his cause; for he would always prefer the answering drive to the lob; he would sooner protect his body and legs than his head. His low volleying is as refined and as effortless as his driving; he has, indeed, a perfect instinct for the game.

VI. *Mrs. Moody.*

Players passing to "the dust and silence of the upper shelf" are not likely to forget the ladies' championship final at Wimbledon in 1927. It was not a long match, neither did its issue waver save for a brief and tense period in the second set. It was remarkable in that the ball was exchanged between the two competitors at a speed hitherto unknown—and by the Victorians probably undreamt of—in woman's play; the drives were man-like in their vigour and challenge.

The two finalists were Miss Helen Wills, of America, and Señorita de Alvarez, of Spain, differing markedly in style and temperament, yet jointly, by their aggressive stroke-play, expressing the evolution of the game as practised by a sex no longer "gentler." Here was the rising ball flogged on either wing with an accuracy both meticulous and sustained, combined with mobility which protected in turn each point of attack, and with a coolness and courage which ignored the excitement of the crowd.

Miss Helen Wills, thrice champion at Wimbledon and unbeaten in any singles match for two years, was not born an artist like two other natives of California—Miss Hazel Hotchkiss (afterwards Mrs. Wightman) and Miss Mary Browne. Her talent only developed through steady and stubborn practice; before it matured her footwork needed the spur of ambition—when I first saw her play it was unusually slow.

But once her zeal was fixed—and at the Berkeley Tennis Club, near San Francisco, the warm daily sunshine is a sure touchstone to enthusiasm—her progress was rapid and even. She played on an average four times a week. Unlike other girls, she did not play, as a rule, more than an hour at a stretch ; and when she had played two hard sets she used any overtime for stroke practice. Thus early did she reveal purpose and a definite goal.

Her physique and temperament were always of great assistance. The first provided service and driving speed over an abnormal period, the second rebuked fear and concealed from an opponent's gaze any mental signal of doubt or annoyance. The American term, "Poker Face," applied to Miss Wills, was egregiously absurd. Her unemotional expression on court was not assumed for any sinister purpose ; it was a natural sign of complete composure. In forty-nine matches out of fifty this sangfroid was valuable and could prove decisive ; in the fiftieth, given unprecedented circumstances, it might conceivably let her down. Thus, if the crowd were, suddenly and without warning, to exhibit an unfriendly bias, the ingrained habit of outward calm might—I do not say would—yield a mental upheaval possibly beyond adequate control. A more volatile personality, like Mr. Tilden or M. Borotra, more liable to pressure from equal opponents, would be more schooled in such crises.

Mrs. Moody has a pure and orthodox style ; in service and drive stroke she is a worthy model for all young girls. Her service is produced with perfect rotation of the body's weight ; the feet are well pivoted, the arms strainlessly swung ; the index finger on the racket's grip gives just the right turn to the racket's face to ensure spin and, therefore, direction and speed on the ball. Her backhand drive is the best woman's backhand drive in the world ; her forehand drive, although not quite as loyal, equally fast and well graded.

As a volleyer her strokes are better than her strategy ; she is for that reason, and because she relies mainly on controlled speed from the back of the court, greater in singles than in doubles. In the former, as her record showed, she has been supreme.

VII. *Señorita de Alvarez.*

In proportion to their numbers women players have provided few champions ; those of transcending skill might almost be counted on the fingers of one hand. This may be the result of a too eager and unapprenticed world ; youth and ardour may take the waiting way of tournament play rather than suffer the greater restraint of patient and private practice. But the fact is there ; the heart and hand are more active than the head in the modern women's game.

Thrice a finalist at Wimbledon, Señorita de Alvarez yet failed to win the crown. On her first and most favourable chance she was beaten by the lady who is now Mrs. Godfree ; in the second and third years by Miss Helen Wills, who afterwards became Mrs. Moody. Yet the champion of Spain had a stroke genius which was admittedly superior to that of her two conquerors. If sets were limited to the best of five games instead to a number of games which may be extended indefinitely, her prospects of victory over either would have found many supporters. For in a restricted break she could be irresistible, a player sweeping all before her, contemptuous of their claim. In the longer match her reactions both of body and mind might bring relief and victory to her opponent.

Adept at physical arts like skating and ski-ing, the Señorita offered to lawn tennis an ease and symmetry of movement making for a natural style. There could be no anatomical strain ; no physical law was abused in stroke production. Her brain, too, had been quickened by cosmopolitan travel. Moreover, initiated and developed on fast continental courts, her game absorbed, and her volatile nature welcomed, the newer method of intercepting the ball on the rise. Short measures and quick returns were always her maxim ; the "knock-out" blow ever her goal. Thus she was found to play most of her drives a definable period before the normal time, to the embarrassment of most of her adversaries and to her own obvious advantage. She even essayed the half-volley on occasions when regard for correct position would suggest a more leisurely, or, at any rate, a more restrained stroke—a penchant which invested her attack with a novelty and daring very pleasing to the crowd.

A brilliant driver on both wings, she was more reliable on her backhand than her forehand, for the former stroke lent itself more readily to her flexible shoulders and wrist. Both these drives carried a measure of top-spin which, while not enough to involve excessive strain in production, added to their value when the ball touched the court. Her service had speed and good length ; it was not always under perfect control. Double faults cost her important games. It may be that by throwing up the ball with the left hand pointing downwards instead of upwards she did not fulfil one of the requisite canons of service.

A complete player, she could volley with skill and decision, but a frontal attack imposed a strain on her stamina none too deep and on a temperament not always proof against vicissitudes. Moreover, she was essentially an individualist, and double harness did not always suit her mood. Even so, she entered for the French doubles championship in 1929 at the eleventh hour with an entirely new partner. She won the event, revealing an adaptability unsuspected by most of the onlookers.

VIII. *Miss E. L. Heine.*

No lady player visiting England for the first time made such a deep impression as Miss Esther L. Heine. She was then only seventeen years of age, and her home in Natal was distant many miles from any court; her practice had been fugitive and her opportunity for match experience rare. But she possessed a natural genius for the game—an instinct for stroke play at once graceful and fluent which only required the spur of competition. Moreover, her footwork was of that character, so valuable in lawn tennis, which permitted either the long stride to rescue the losing and distant ball or the short dovetailing step so important for a volleyer in a restricted space.

On her first arrival in England in 1927, Miss Heine defeated Señorita de Alvarez in Paris and reached the final of the doubles at Wimbledon. At both these championships, as elsewhere, she revealed a temperament proof against passing misfortune and effectively serene in a crisis—a legacy, no doubt, of the environment of the open veldt. The same imperturbability which Australian players also reveal saved Miss Heine from disaster in the final of the British hard-court championship at Bournemouth. She was then four times within a stroke of defeat by Miss Ridley; on each occasion her good faerie held her up.

Overhead, and on the backhand, Miss Heine was as good as any player in the tournament lists. Her smash, short or deep, was perfectly timed; only the best lob could cheat her of a decisive blow. Her backhand volley down the line was her best stroke, and a shot which no other player of her sex achieved with the same skill. Had she a little more pace on her ground shots—and the ability to obtain it was there—she might have employed her volleying powers more profitably in singles. But she developed a tendency to fence at the back of the court; she became less aggressive on the drive. As a result her volleying had less scope; the element of surprise was not used enough.

She shows greater mobility and more variety of stroke than Mrs. Moody; a surer instinct for the game than any lady player since Mlle Lenglen. Perhaps she needs more pace on her forehand drive and a greater determination to shorten the rally. Lawn tennis came to her so naturally that she probably does not put quite enough iron into her spirit. She does not attack as often as she might.

CHAPTER
FOURTEEN

COURTS AND COURT-MAKING

CHAPTER FOURTEEN

COURTS AND COURT-MAKING

OF the making of courts, as of books, there is no end, and their quality is as infinite. The laws of the game, common to all countries, may define and impose uniform measurements ; in surface conditions they have never attempted to exact parity. Nor would legislation prescribing a standardised court be possible, for all outdoor courts must be influenced by the climate of their locality and will differ both in endurance and in the manner in which they receive the ball—itself, by the way, of a variable type, the flight dependent both on the date and method of its manufacture.

Even in places experiencing the same weather, no groups of courts can be relied upon to yield identical conditions. In Cannes, on the French Riviera, for example, there are five clubs the courts of which, although superficially of the same character, all offer a different reception in pace and bound to the same strokes—an inconsistency which will affect the play even of the expert. If local courts, favoured by the same climate, have these conflicting attributes, it must pass the wit of man to guarantee a surface that shall provide the same playing conditions in all, or even in two, countries. Were the resources for that purpose available—were it possible for British turf to flourish in all countries or for the ant-heap of the Transvaal to be a cheap and accessible mineral in England—exact uniformity could not be ensured unless every court was backgrounded in the same way and every game took place in the same atmosphere and light. That ideal is not for the tennis player, not would he be happy to see it realised. The historian may suggest that the game would never have distributed its nationals over the world if every country had the same playing conditions. The cynic may add that the invader has often pleaded unfamiliar surface and surroundings as the only cause of his defeat.

The relative merits of particular courts is a theme for

frequent discussion. As a rule, the debater votes for the surface which favours his own game, regardless of the fact that until a new surface has been given more than a fugitive trial it cannot be compared with a familiar floor. The grass courts of Wimbledon, their pace affected by the weather, depressed the spirit of the French invader until, after several visits, he realised that its cushion-like plane was the best medium for expressing the refined art at which he excelled. There was less resistance both to the foot and to the ball than that encountered on his home courts of burnt clay and wood. Whether for aggressive or defensive play, or for a combination of both, firm and true turf will always remain the natural surface for lawn tennis ; and of all its manifold substitutes, which supply an aggregate of courts far exceeding that of grass courts, there is none which the really great player, inured to turf conditions, would select in preference. Its utility for club and household purposes is another matter. Its season is limited to a few months in the year, and its demand for constant and expert attention, which may often be lacking, give its artificial competitors an opening they have been quick to seize. But it would be fallacious to claim for hard courts of the oversea pattern, admirable as these have proved for training young players, any sovereign virtue for producing champions. For the first twenty-seven years of its existence the international championship, symbolised in the Davis Cup, was held by a country holding its own championships on grass courts ; the French players who finally broke that record owed their advance mainly to their turf-court-match experience in England and America.

Turf Courts.

Some advice on the construction of a grass court, supplied by the leading authority, Mr. Reginald Beale, F.L.S., author of *Lawns for Sports*, follows.

An area of 120 by 60 feet is desirable. Since the actual doubles court is 78 by 36 feet, this space will allow 21 feet for the run-back and 12 feet for the side-run. To avoid playing into the rising or setting sun, the court should be laid north to south. N.N.W. to S.S.E. is the orientation of the centre court at Wimbledon, which, by the way, has a run-back of 26 feet and a side-run of 23 feet 3 inches.

Levelling is the first task. The fall of the ground can easily be ascertained with a series of pegs, a straight-edge, and a spirit-level. If a peg is fixed in the highest point, protruding, say, 6 inches from the surface in order to clear obstructions, and the one in the lower point is 6 feet 6 inches above the existing level—it is clear that the ground will have to be excavated at the high end to a depth of 3 feet, and made up 3 feet at the lower end. If the ground falls both ways, it will be necessary to take cross levels; when these are got out any labouring man can work to them. If the alteration is so serious as to render any danger from a steep bank, the court should be extended by 6 feet or more. Existing turf should not be destroyed; if stacked in a convenient place to rot, it can be used in the making of compost. The top spit of soil should be removed and placed on one side. This is important, especially if the surface soil be thin and the subsoil of a poor gravel or clay. If the surface soil be lost or badly mixed with the undesirable subsoil, satisfactory results afterwards will be more difficult and costly.

The operation of levelling, of wheeling the subsoil from the high end and dumping it on the lower, must be done with great care. The subsoil should be spread evenly in thin layers and well trodden down in position, otherwise it will settle and spoil the playing surface. Settlement is almost certain if the make-up exceed 18 inches or if the soil is at all stiff. Then there are only two alternatives—to finish off the court with the full intention of re-levelling it later, or to level it in the rough for a year and then to re-level and finish it off.

Unless the subsoil is of a porous nature—that is, not of a retentive or clayey character—drainage will be necessary. No hard-and-fast rule can be laid down; the man on the spot will have to use his discretion. But if the court has been levelled in the way described, the excavated end will have received the surface water running from the hill and oozing out of the banks. It is therefore prudent in all cases to cut two trenches along the top end at the foot of the banks, making them about 12 inches deep at their junction and 18 inches at their ends. If necessary, a similar trench should be cut diagonally across the court, allowing a fall in its length of at least 18 inches. Three-inch pipes should be laid down in all drains; cinders should be used to fill up. This triangular drain will catch any surface water that may flow on to the court from a higher ground or ooze out of the banks. Additional spurs may be added if required. When dealing with heavy, impervious clays it is imperative to spread a layer of ashes from 3 to 6 inches deep over the whole site. If there is any possibility of surface water from the higher ground flooding the lawn, it should be cut off by digging a diagonal ditch or trench across the face of the hill. Level sites should be drained on the herring-bone principle, with a 4-inch drain down the centre and 3-inch spurs, 12, 15, or 20 feet apart, according to circumstances; but if the site is likely to be wet, it will be better in the long run to excavate it 12 inches deep, and to put in a moderate system consisting of, say, a 4-inch main down the centre and 3-inch spurs 20 to 30 feet apart, and cover it with a 3-inch to 6-inch layer of ashes.

The ideal soil for a turf court is good fibrous loam; it will carry a fine, strong, hard-wearing turf possessing a firm, true surface that will not readily break up or crumble under foot. If the local soil does not answer to this description, sufficient should be purchased to form a layer over the entire site from 1 to 6 inches deep. A cube yard of soil weighs about 14 cwt. For an area of 800 square yards the approximate quantity of soil required would vary from 25 cube yards for a 1-inch layer to 150 cube yards for a 6-inch layer. Of course, if purchased soil be used, a similar quantity of the natural soil will have to be discarded.

Whatever class of soil is considered—and it may often be decided to use the existing soil—there should be a test for lime—easily carried out with a Carter Lime-Testing Outfit. Healthy grass must have sufficient lime; without it no satisfactory result can be obtained. Pulverised chalk at the rate of 1 lb. per square yard may be used to supply the deficiency.

Light sands are not a desirable class of soil. They dry out quickly, crumble underfoot, and can only carry a fine, starved turf. If, however, they are well manured, and regularly watered, fertilised, and top-dressed, they can be worked up to give good results. Gravels are usually deficient in lime and are fiery; they pack closely and arrest the quick, natural movements of the moisture in the soil. They should be treated in the same way as sands unless they contain an undesirable quantity of stone, when the ground should be broken up at least 6 inches deep and sifted with a sieve or screen with an appropriate mesh before adding the lime or manure. Chalk, because of its sticky and binding nature, is a difficult soil. It should be broken up, and to every 100 square yards of the surface should be added 1 yard or more of fine cinders passed through a ¼-inch square mesh sieve. One or two loads of well-rotted short straw manure should be added. Loams are the easiest soils and the best from all points of view. Clays should always be built on a cinder foundation, the soil well broken up and thoroughly mixed with fine cinders or sand, using 2 to 3 cube yards or more per 100 square yards. By using cinders, heavy or clay soil will be opened up, the surface drainage will be improved, the soil warmed, and the roots of the grass given easier access.

Every load of material used in the making of a court should be spread evenly and well trodden into position. Breeze, if used, should be thoroughly mixed with the soil right the way through; all manure should be incorporated with the surface soil and none of it buried deeper than 3 inches. The same depth and quality of soil throughout will thus be insured. The danger point is always at the excavated end. If the drainage or top-soiling has been neglected or skimped, the turf will be wet or mossy; it will be exceedingly difficult to improve it afterwards without considerable expense.

Time must be the factor in choosing either turf or seed. If turf of good quality is put down, the court will be ready in the following spring. But, of course, it is more expensive than seed; nor can the absence of weed be guaranteed. Turf free from weeds does not exist commercially, while if not laid in time to ensure ample water it may die; as much attention must be given it as to the sown lawn. Cumberland turf is the best available, but its cost, with railway charges, is heavy. A square yard of turf cut 1½ inches thick weighs about 112 lb.; the turf required for a regulation court, with its area of 800 square yards, would weigh 40 tons. Down, Heath, or Moorland turf requires local knowledge of selection. Meadow turf is usually of inferior quality, full of weeds, coarse grasses, and dormant weed seed. Time and proper treatment will be necessary before it can be worked up.

Turf should be cut 12 by 12 by 2 inches and, if possible, trimmed in a gauge-box to a thickness of 1½ inches. It can thus be laid accurately on a firm, true surface without packing. Whatever class of turf is used, weeds will be found; it is much easier to remove them before laying. Each sod should therefore be placed on a rough bench, brushed, and carefully picked over before it is laid. It is a mistake when laying to beat the turf heavily, particularly if the soil is of a tenacious character. The turf should be dressed with finely sifted soil mixed with a little grass seed

—about 4 lb. of seed to a barrow-load of soil ; this should be worked well in and between the cracks with the back of a wooden rake or a birch broom.

If the turf is laid in the autumn, it should be rolled periodically, when the weather is neither too wet nor too dry, with a light wooden roller ; later it should be brushed with a stiff birch broom, and then, to remove the old foliage as quick as possible, mowed with a machine set as low as possible. Worms should be destroyed at the earliest moment ; in all cases weeding should be carefully carried out. Turf may be worked into playing condition by dressing it every second or third week with quarter-dressings, ½ ounce to the square yard, of No. 1 Fertiliser and soil or compost, well mixed together and finely sifted, provided the weather is open and showery or water is available. As the turf develops a heavier roller may be used ; it should be drawn by hand alternately across the length and width of the ground.

If seed be chosen in preference to turf, the best time for sowing is from mid-August to mid-September. The soil is warm at the end of the summer, and both rain and dew, causing rapid and even germination, may be expected. The young grass has time to become well established before the cold weather arrives. Moreover, weeds are more prevalent in spring than in autumn ; autumn-sown grass will be better able to withstand the onslaught of weeds.

When the ground is prepared for a dead true, firm surface, it should be divided up into strips or squares of equal area, marked by pegs and string. The seed should be sown by hand at the minimum rate of 1 ounce or the maximum rate of 2 ounces per square yard, care being taken to spread it evenly over the surface. After sowing, the strings should be removed and the ground raked and cross-raked to a depth of about ¼ inch, thus covering the seed as much as possible. A light roller should then be applied. The whole of the work should be done on a dry day when the soil will not stick to the boots nor pick up on the roller.

The young grass should appear above the ground in 5 to 10 days, if autumn-sown, and in 14 to 21 days if spring-sown, according to the weather. It is better to make the first cutting with a sharp scythe, but when the grass is about 1 inch high it may be cut with a sharp, free-acting machine, set rather high. Weeds must be removed before they get firmly established. After the first mowing the young grass can be hardened into growth by dressing with Malt Culms, Carter's Compound Mulch, or quarter dressings of Fertiliser mixed with freely sifted soil or compost. As the young grass closes up and gains in strength the knives of the mowing machine should be set lower; it may then be mowed and rolled regularly, and generally kept in playing condition until it is strong enough for actual play. But until that day arrives, and after it, the court must be carefully tended.

For the bare patches which will come as a result of wear and tear during the season, especially on the baselines, repair in the autumn is absolutely essential. The turf has not only been destroyed root and blade, but an actual depression has probably worn in the soil. To avoid delay, preparation should be made well in advance; seeds, fertilisers, and other materials should be ready. All bare places should be repaired and levelled with good, strong, fibrous turf, weeded clear before laying. The turf must either be purchased or taken from the sides or backs of the court. In the latter case the stripped area should at once be made good with well-prepared soil and sown heavily to ensure recovery by next season. The fertiliser should be added at the rate of 2 ounces per square yard, mixed with two to four barrow-loads of soil, the mixture screened with the object of stopping undesirable matter. When ordering grass seed, by the way, it is advisable to send a specimen sample of the turf.

Under the wear and tear of modern play nearly all grass courts require a certain measure of summer feeding. Nature is throwing up its seed heads to reproduce itself; it revolts against the mower and the traffic of players. Not only is the plant exhausted but the chemical constituents of the soil perish. Mr. Beale estimates that 1 ton of grass removes from the soil 34 lbs. of nitrogen, 36 lbs. of potash, and 16 lbs. of phosphoric acid. Thus robbed of its normal nourishment, the turf needs an artificial stimulant to maintain its strength. If it is fed gently during the season, it will not wear as badly or as rapidly. Provided the turf is in growth and the weather showery, summer feeding may be done at any time. The application is quarter doses of half an ounce per square yard of Complete Fertiliser. This should be well mixed with three or four times its own bulk of compost soil or sand, the whole finely sifted to ensure even distribution. A Graduated Distributor may be used, and the mixture brushed in with a birch broom or light bush harrow, allowing an interval of at least a fortnight between the dressings. Summer feeding need not interfere with play. It presents the only chance of keeping turf in good condition if it is much used.

Courts may be kept "dead" level if all top-dressings are worked across it by means of a straight-edge about 10 feet long, 9 inches high, and 1 inch or more wide, with rounded ends. Finely sifted compost should be placed in front of the straight edge and spread over the lawn by working it from left to right and forward at the same time; sufficient quantity should escape beneath the straight edge to fill up the little hollows. Small humps and hollows can be corrected by making an + + incision in the turf, enabling it to be rolled back so that soil may be added or taken away as may be required before the turf is replaced.

In regard to background, a yew hedge 6 to 9 feet high may be recommended. All that is needed is 120 3-foot yews. Planted in properly prepared ground, mixing rotted dung with the soil at the rate of 1 load per 10 or 20 yards' run, they should grow on an average at least 9 inches each year. Growth can be increased if the ground on each side of the hedge is kept open to a width of 18 to 24 inches, and cultivated and mulched with well-rotted dung and fertilised with dry blood. Iron or wood standards 9 feet high, braced together with four lines of strong galvanised iron wire, the first fixed at ground level and the others 3 feet apart, and the whole covered with fish or galvanised-iron netting securely laced into position, are the most suitable for club use. It is desirable to have independent entrances to each court. Nothing is more disconcerting to players than that their back or side runs should be crossed by other players aiming to reach their courts.

Hard or Artificial Courts.

Lawn tennis was played on a surface other than turf in its earliest days; indeed, the twin Renshaws, who are entitled to be called its Fathers, not only learnt the game on asphalt courts but, visiting Cannes in the early 'eighties, were the pioneers of hard courts on the Continent. The notion that non-turf courts in Great Britain are, in relation to the game's history, of modern introduction has no substance.

Scotland had many hard courts in the nineteenth century, and Scotch Blaes was a conventional floor for match play. Scotch Blaes was obtained from the pit banks, and was a mixture of burnt clay and coal ash deposited after combustion. It was quite a useful material, but one of its chief drawbacks was that different kinds of material got mixed and burnt together in the heap. One part of the court would drain and be comparatively loose; another part would be slow in drainage and very firm. The burnt ashes from the coal deposits would constitute the first parts and the clay would constitute the second. But the hardy sportsmen of the North made light of this defect; they enjoyed their games thoroughly.

But useful as these courts proved for "keeping in the hand and eye" during what was regarded then as the close season, they lacked resiliency and pace; most of them were tiring to the feet and were inclined to discolour the balls; and the work of repair after premature settlement or the ravages of frost was long and expensive. In 1909 Commander G. W. Hillyard, R.N., returned from South Africa, where he had been touring with an All-England Club team, much impressed with the ant-heap courts laid down freely in that country. Experiments were made with Leicestershire clay, specially treated. A new type of court, which was to revolutionise court-making in this country and to gain increasing customers abroad, was constructed on a foundation made approximately of 6 inches of mixed ashes at the bottom, rising to fine ash on the surface. On this was placed about 1 inch of the special type of clay, burnt in kilns to an even hardness, which kept the surface uniform for pace, drainage, and firmness. The court was voted a great advance on any other outdoor court previously tested; it proved to be the beginning of hard-court making as a commercial enterprise; the company which introduced it put down twelve thousand courts within the next twenty years.

Speaking generally, hard courts to-day are of two classes—those of the adamant variety, and those of the semi-loose or resilient type. The former are either made of concrete, asphalt, or granite mixed with bitumen, and some of the best of them are quite good for Public Parks, where they are treated as playgrounds as well as courts. They have also been found serviceable in places which have no water for upkeep purposes, even though this difficulty is now overcome by makers of some of the more advanced types of semi-loose or resilient courts. The disadvantages of the adamant variety are that they are often expensive to make, and if the site has had to be levelled there is risk of the surface either cracking or sinking. If this once occurs, it is most difficult to repair properly. They are also tiring to play on, especially on a hot day; they are apt to blister the feet.

Of the resilient or semi-loose type of court those made from burnt clay are probably in the majority. They vary materially in quality, but that may be as much the fault of the owner as of the contractor. It is very important to have this type of court made from clay evenly burnt, since it is necessary in regard to evenness of colour, hardness of surface, and equal drainage, that the surface shall not weather back to its natural state of clay in a few years. Methods are now adopted by some of the best known makers by which two or more kinds of clay are burnt for the purpose. One is a clay that gives a deep dark red colour when burnt; it is so hard that it will not weather back for a long period, although kept in a state of continuous moisture. On the other hand, this type of clay is not too good for binding, and therefore the makers burn and mix evenly another type of clay that is not quite so good from a drainage point of view but is an admirable binder; it keeps the surface tight and firm, enabling fast play to be obtained. To get a temporary bind, until moisture and rolling has its effect on the clay, a liquid has been found which will consolidate the materials until heavy rains gradually wash it through into the ash foundation.

Red-surface courts are also made out of shale from the pit banks. These bind together very quickly. The shale, however, may be unevenly burnt and, what is more, may vary in character; these courts tend to become sticky and drain badly. Moss and other vegetation are thus encouraged.

Other courts are made from granites or gravels. The former, as a rule, is put on the surface to the size of about one-eighth of an inch, including dust, and the weight of the granite, with watering and rolling, will give a satisfactory surface which requires very little upkeep. Being heavy, it does not blow away; and being sharp, it gives a fairly good foothold. But the floor is tiring to the feet. In time atmospheric dirt settles on the court or dust blows on to it; the surface becomes sluggish and slow in draining.

A not unjust criticism of red-surface courts is that they become loose and dusty. Experiments with new types of clay have produced better results. Especially noteworthy has been the success of the type of court used for the French championships at Auteuil—a surface which, in the absence of rain or artificial watering, actually hardens and improves. This material has been introduced into England with beneficial results, and by mixing with it some of the finest home-burnt clays a darker colour has been secured. This court may be commended for spring or autumn play; in winter it does not recover quickly after frost.

A type of court made in some districts is composed of dust from slate quarries. Some of the slate from the Westmorland quarries is more or less green when moist, but it is very light grey when the surface gets dry. The disadvantage of this class of court is that when the surface is dry it is too light and does not give a contrast between ball and court—nor can the baselines be seen easily—while in wet weather the surface may become sticky.

Most of the semi-loose or resilient types of court cost approximately £120, assuming a level site free from turf is offered to the maker, and that ashes for the foundation can be delivered to the site at 5s. per cubic yard. Wire-netting surrounds, marking tapes, and posts and nets are, of course, extras.

The adamant type either of the concrete or asphalt variety, cost, as a general rule, from £300 to £350 per court on a level site, assuming foundation material can be obtained at 5s. per cubic yard. No marking tapes are required for this class of court.

Marking tapes are used on most of the semi-loose or resilient courts, with the exception of the Paris court, on which the lines can be painted if play is only desired in spring, summer, or autumn. If the court is wanted for use during the periods between frosts, it is necessary to have marking tapes fixed, for the painted lines will crack in frosty weather.

There is little or no upkeep on asphalt or concrete courts, but to keep the surface green it is necessary to re-spray at least once a year. The upkeep of a semi-loose or resilient court is to roll it and water it when it gets too dry; once a year to give it a little top dressing to make good any low places; and to take off the grit and restore a fine clean surface. This work depends on the type of court put down, but the best known courts vary very little in maintenance. The French court previously mentioned requires little or no rolling in hot weather; it hardens in the sun and requires only a surface sprinkling to settle the surface dust. Other resilient types require well soaking in hot weather and more frequent rolling.

Certain rules are common to the construction of all outdoor hard courts. The site should not be chosen in any depression. Water from higher ground will always find its way to a lower level ; nothing seems to attract it more rapidly than a tennis court. Of course it is essential that there should be no shadow across the playing area ; trees are movable but masonry is not. A green or black background is to be preferred ; even trees at a distance may, when the sun reaches their level, prove objectionable. Remember, too, that a sand or kindred surface is relatively tender and will not stand harsh treatment. A brush that is too hard or a roller that is too heavy can do positive harm. Never throw sand over a court promiscuously, especially when it is wet. A sand that does not bind will give a false bound ; loose sand has that defect. Finally, do not expect that an outdoor court, whatever contractors may say—and the best makers do not advance that claim—will be available for play every day of the year. If it is, then it has been neglected, for it cannot have received its essential care.

Covered Courts.

Covered courts divide themselves into three independent categories—those erected for private owners, courts for first-class clubs, and courts for the use of municipalities.

Even in the case of private courts the architect rarely has a free hand in regard to cost. More often than not, when he places the original estimate before his client, he is told that the cost is prohibitive ; at best it is accepted with the strict injunction that no extras must occur. Sometimes, as the work progresses, the owner wishes that he had made it more in accord with his surrounding property or rather more ornate in external appearance, even though its cost would thereby be increased.

In comparing estimates for a court it is necessary to ensure that they are uniform in essentials. Every court for a private owner must be of a size suitable for first-class play. It must have an area of glass which in winter will give the maximum light without letting in the sun's rays at too low an angle. The structure must constitute not a mere covering ; it must give a feeling to the players that it is a building erected and suitable for its particular purpose. Where the building is steel, self-supported, it must be calculated to the proper factor of safety. The materials utilised must be such as to demand the minimum of upkeep, and be reasonably pleasing both in external and internal appearances.

These factors have been carefully considered in the standard design for a covered court which is the copyright of Mr. P. M. Davson, F.R.I.B.A., Chartered Architect, and covered-court champion in 1913 and 1919. His design is the outcome of the consideration of some fifty-five different schemes for covered courts.

The building is a steel self-supporting structure. The roof, where not glazed, is finished in russet brown asbestos tiles. The walls are built in terra-cotta blocks—materials which are in the same category. When the owner desires to make appearances coincide with the buildings on his property, the same tiles and filling utilised in the latter can be substituted, the cost, of course, increasing proportionately.

Some owners like only a few doors—two on each side; others prefer large folding doors which leave two-thirds of each side open. Where a court is to be heated the smaller doors may be recommended.

The floor surface is a matter of choice. Those who are familiar with continental play prefer a hard-court surface, to which they are accustomed. Those who play on covered courts in England almost invariably prefer wood. The courts at Queen's Club are of American whitewood, which is advantageous because it has no knots, and gives rather a faster surface than deal. But it is expensive, and probably pitch pine, rift grain, would prove equally good and less expensive. A surface that is utilised in America is Battleship linoleum, but this is very little less expensive than wood.

A small gallery at one end of the court is usually demanded. The lobby entrance forms the entrance to the court, and a staircase from the lobby leads to the gallery. Covered courts can be heated by hot water on the radiator system, hot air, or by hot water on a patent panel system with overhead panels and exposed pipes in the roof. A Robin Hood or similar boiler would be required, with all necessary fittings, including an electrically driven pump and motor to maintain circulation through the pipes.

Adjuncts to covered courts in the form of a squash court and a swimming-bath have been modern developments. A squash court can be constructed upon similar lines and of similar materials as the covered court. It will be, of course, to standard size, 32 feet by 21 feet. The floor should be of hard wood, preferably maple. The best finish for the walls is to render them in cement. Attention to several details in connection with the playboard, entrance door, lighting, etc., are necessary if the court is to afford the pleasure that it can and does now yield to a very large number.

An economic scheme for municipalities is probably to have three covered hard lawn tennis courts with large folding-doors. These doors increase the cost, but it has been proved that throughout the summer, except on the very hottest days, a breeze passes through them and renders play quite pleasant. Another advantage of three courts is that temporary stands can be put up on one or both sides for the final day of a tournament or for important matches.

The cost of three covered hard courts with large folding-doors, including the specialised surface, would be approximately £10,000. The general charge for municipal open-air hard courts is about 1s. 6d. per hour. It would, of course, be impossible at first to get the playing fee down to that figure, but at popular health resorts a fee of 4s. per hour could probably be obtained. Covered courts are often used for seven periods of 1¼ hours per day for eight months of the year. Revenue for municipal covered courts (with large doors) might, therefore, be based upon nine periods of one hour per day eight months of the year. Upon this basis a revenue of about £1300 would be obtainable from court fees, and another £100 from tournaments and matches, making £1400 in all. Against this must be set the interest on the capital expenditure of £10,000—say £600. This leaves £800 per annum to cover upkeep and additional attendance to courts, rates and taxes, lighting, water and insurance. A small profit on the year's working should, therefore, be shown for the first five years. A sinking fund might subsequently be established to pay off the capital in about twenty years.

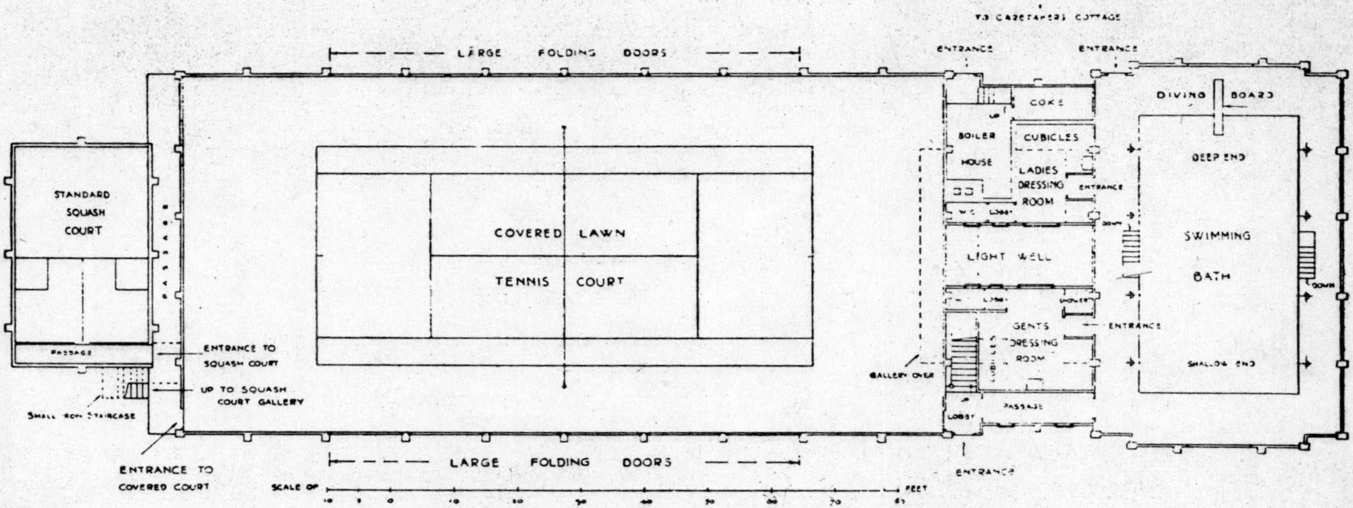

Fig. 5.

DESIGN FOR A COVERED COURT AND ADJUNCTS.

APPROXIMATE COSTS OF COVERED COURTS OF SIZES AND LENGTH SUITABLE TO FIRST-CLASS PLAY

	One Court.	Two Courts side by side.	Three Courts side by side.
1. Structure *only*, assuming level site, normal foundations, and including drainage and flat type roof truss (four doors), all woodwork Solignum finish . .	£3000	£5500	£8000
2. *Add* to No. 1 for hard court surface including water supply, netting and supports at back and over doors, nets, and posts, etc., complete	£260	£450	£650
3. *Add* to No. 1 for wood court with deal floor, including painting wall and floor green	£792	£1584	£2376

4. *Add* "per court" to No. 1 for curved roof trusses, giving better appearance . . . . 5 per cent.

5. *Add* to totals of No. 1 if stanchions are cased instead of being left exposed and painted £100

6. *Add* "per court" if roof is painted instead of left plain £80

7. *Add* to total of No. 1, if six folding doors each side, leaving two-third sides of courts open, with best quality opening fittings and extra netting and supports are provided (instead of two small sliding doors each side) £420

8. *Add* "per court" to totals of No. 3 if American whitewood is substituted over playing area £232

9. *Add* for small gallery at end, with lobby entrance to court and staircase approach (according to size) . . £250 to £380

10. *Add* for radiator heating installation for *one* court, including boiler pump, electric motor, and builder's work in connection £1007

11. *Add* for complete independent lighting plant for *one* court, with wiring, lamps, and 100 feet of cable (but exclusive of engine house) £996

Note.—Wiring and lamps only for fully efficient lighting installation.

12. *Add* to (cost of) three courts for dressing-room accommodation, with large card-room, bar, and gallery, 48′ 0″ × 3′ 0″ wide £1000

13. In order to arrive at approximate total outlay, add 6 per cent. (except lighting, 2 per cent. only) to the total arrived at from the above figures for architect's fees.

These approximate costs are, of course, subject to slight variations according to the district in which the courts are constructed.

Artificial Lighting of Courts.

The essentials of a satisfactory scheme of lighting for covered courts are :

1. A good light over the playing area.
2. Absence of glare to the eye of the player.
3. Moderate cost in current consumption.

After a great number of comparative tests, a scheme of lighting which has been found satisfactory is the Allom System. Some fourteen to sixteen 500-watt units of high efficiency are used with multiple parabola reflectors constructed of a series of bent glass sections ; and with sixteen arranged in one straight line down the centre of the court

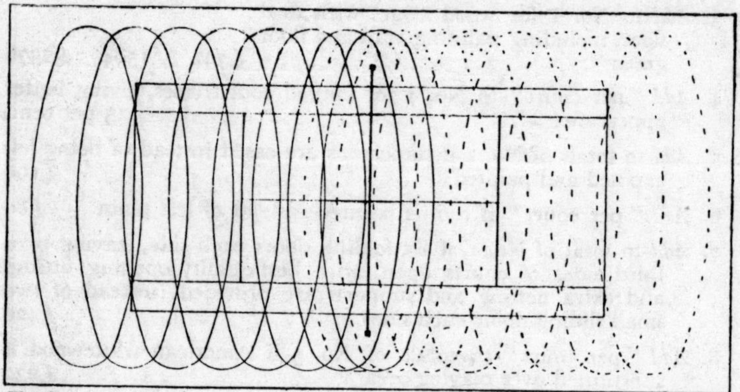

Fig. 6.

PLAN OF LIGHTING FOR A COVERED COURT.

at a height of 30 to 32 feet, the whole of the playing area is covered.

Fig. 6 shows the plan with the sixteen beams, each being wide enough to cover the area of play across the court, and to give smooth and uniform distribution, with the stronger light down the centre, graduating off to a 20 per cent. reduction down the side-lines. This gives the highest intensity of illumination for the fastest travelling balls.

Fig. 7 shows a longitudinal section down the centre of the court. It will be observed that the beams of light are directed towards the net, so that the service and overhead smash can be effected without glare to the eye of the player.

The fitting is constructed for a standard gas-filled lamp,

with a suspension which can be adjusted to direct the beam as required, so that uniformity of light can be obtained.

Some courts have been lighted with as few as eleven to twelve of these 500-watt units, but fourteen to sixteen should be used. With the latter the current consumption is 8 units per hour, giving a photometric reading of fifteen to twenty foot candles over the area of play at four feet from the ground. With the fittings suspended in a straight line down the centre of the court, the installation of wiring is simplified.

Accessibility is an important factor. Lamps are liable to lose efficiency, and it is, therefore, desirable to replace them quickly. If a cumbersome ladder, necessitating

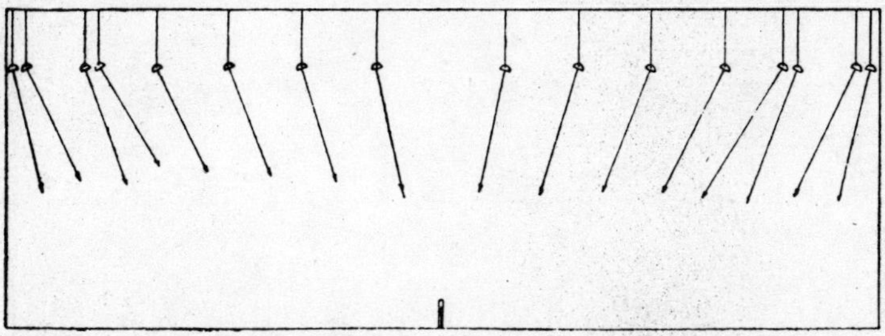

Fig. 7.

ELEVATION OF LIGHTING FOR A COVERED COURT.

three or four hands, is the only means of access, faulty lighting, in consequence of the trouble of changing a lamp, frequently results. A simple and inexpensive scheme of suspension has been designed for raising and lowering the fittings, consisting of pulleys and jute-covered steel wires, so that a lamp can be replaced while the players are waiting on the court.

Artificial lighting of outdoor courts has proved a practical proposition, especially in America, where both side and overhead systems have been introduced with success. It is claimed by American business men that the pleasure derived from night playing is a return on the expenditure involved.

CHAPTER
FIFTEEN

THE RACKET AND THE BALL

CHAPTER FIFTEEN

THE RACKET AND THE BALL

THE rules of lawn tennis, unlike those of other games in which a ball is struck by an instrument, make no prescriptions as to the size, weight, or quality of the racket. Those attributes are entirely at the discretion of the player. He would be defying convention but not the legislators if he took into court an implement entirely abnormal in character. The historian would be a little perplexed by the lacuna did he not realise that the lawn tennis racket is a lineal descendant of the racket used for the royal and ancient game of tennis. Modern rackets may disguise that derivation successfully ; in its earliest days the game was pursued with a racket which paid fealty to its honoured ancestor.

The evolution of the racket may be observed from the accompanying illustrations. The pioneers of lawn tennis, in grafting a scion of one tree on to another, naturally employed shapes and weights both in the handle and in the head with which they were familiar ; and it may be hazarded that, when experimenting with the new culture, they had no conception, even in their dreams, of its wide-world development. The rackets of the first era could not be made by any regulation pattern, for none existed ; they were mainly the creation of makers who were feeling their way with a new and possibly an ephemeral pastime. Accordingly there were two distinct classes—rackets of excellent material and of fine and careful workmanship (as specimens preserved sixty years afterwards revealed), which were usually ordered specially by patrons of the game and followed a design favoured by the owner; and rackets of a cheaper kind manufactured to catch what was then regarded as a passing breeze of favour.

Those who first played lawn tennis, as earlier chapters have demonstrated, borrowed their style, as they borrowed their implements, from tennis. The ball was cut diagonally over a net which, tapering towards the centre, excluded side-line driving ; the overhead service had not been conceived, and volleying was then regarded as an impertinent experiment—scarcely "cricket." For this limited exercise the racket with the curved or pear-shaped head was deemed suitable if not indispensable. The broadening of the face followed the requirements of wider stroke play ; as the net became more uniform in height, and the resources of the service and the volleying art were exploited, the racket was reconstructed in sympathy. Generally speaking, evolution has followed stroke development ; no legislative authority has ever attempted to fetter it. Modern manufacturers have concentrated their skill and enterprise on strengthening a frame which will meet the increasing demands of speed and action, as well as the rigours and variations of climate. Coloured shoulder-bands was a detail of fashion unrelated to the science of the game.

The earlier rackets illustrated in this volume must not be regarded as marking a period definitely associated with and limited to their reign. Champions of the 'eighties, like the Renshaws and Lawford, held personal views on details of construction, and requested makers to carry them out ; these players did not consider the fashion of the hour. The precise date when the lop-sided racket disappeared from tournament play is therefore difficult to affirm ; for an appreciable period the straight head and the curved were seen on court together.

The following notes may be appended to the pictures in their order :

1. The parent racket, used for tennis.
2. A racket made in 1877 by Buchanan of Piccadilly and called the "Horace Bailey." The foreman to the makers was Thomas J. Tate, who afterwards became the most famous maker of his day.
3. A racket made by Slazengers about 1881. Its head is straighter and the handle is built up.
4. An early Tate racket, made in 1882. The "throw off" is almost entirely eliminated ; the gut is particularly strong and heavy.
5. Another and straighter Tate, made for Mr. Ernest Renshaw in 1883. The handle is much larger.
6. One of the original Demon rackets, made in 1885. It has a square head, a four-piece frame, and a fish-tailed handle. It is strung with "18-strand gut," which was a feature of the year.

7. The racket, dated 1897, with which Mr. R. F. Doherty won his first championship. His signature, written in ink, appears on the frame. It was designed after many experiments by Mr. E. G. Meers. It was longer and narrower than earlier rackets.
8. The racket designed two years later (1899) by Mr. R. F. Doherty and made by Slazengers to his instructions. It had double strings in the centre to give it extra driving powers ; also strengthened shoulders.
9. One of several special rackets produced in the early 'nineties to give extra strength and elasticity. It is made partly of ash and partly of malacca cane.
10. The modern " Queen's " racket made by Slazengers. Its rounded frame is of finely selected English ash. Single strung with all-white gut, the extra trebbling in both directions ensures a minimum displacement of main and cross strings. The shoulders are especially reinforced and bound in pale blue.
11. Another modern racket—the Spalding " Top-Flight." The head is lighter and smaller, permitting very tight stringing. The patent shoulder reinforcement gives strength for many re-stringings. The throat is open, with a view to improving balance and giving greater driving power and resilience.

The resistance of gut both to the wear and tear of strenuous play and to the vagaries of weather must necessarily vary. The modern champion may use a new racket every week, or at least have several spare rackets at hand. Champions of the past were less fastidious, nor did their play appear to suffer. It is the man behind the racket that will always count.

The evolution of the ball, in every particular save shape, has been drastic ; here, again, the developments of modern play have dictated policy. The earliest ball, of grey rubber, was $2\frac{1}{4}$ inches in diameter. But the rubber was very thin ; it had neither the width nor the strength of the modern stické ball, which it otherwise resembled. The first covering, suggested by Mr. J. M. Heathcote in 1874, was of wash leather, cut in two sections like the figure eight. These sections were oversewn with plain thread and then herringbone stitched in addition with coloured silk, red appearing on one side of the seam and blue on the other. Three years later, just before the first championship meeting, Mr. F. H. Ayres covered balls with white and coloured felts. This material was not the woven cloth used for the modern ball, but really a felt, and the thickness was approximately that of the cloth subsequently employed. These balls were oversewn in the same way as the wash-leather-covered balls and decorated with herringbone stitching. Owing to some trouble with the cutting of the thread stitches, catgut sewing was tried, but the experiment did not survive very long. Experiments were also made with twill and canvas coverings.

In March 1877 a Mr. Buchanan took out a provisional patent for covering rubber balls with flannel or felt and attaching the cover by means of solution. He had been anticipated, however, by Mr. Ayres, who had already begun to cement or solution covers. At first the solution was placed on the middle of the sections and not all round the edges as well. Stitching was relied upon to keep the covers from lifting.

In 1879 the size of the ball was regulated and its diameter increased to 2½ inches; these larger balls were made with felt coverings and cemented in the same way as the smaller balls. In 1880 the regulation balls were covered for the first time with a woven melton cloth, and were sold both with stitched covers and with cemented covers only without any stitching.

Very little change occurred for the next three years, although it was found, especially on asphalt courts, that hard play tended to cut the outside stitches. Mr. Ayres finally triumphed by stitching through the thickness of the cloth, and the advent of his undersewn ball proved to be a timely and revolutionary invention. In 1884 the first consignment of balls with "the imperceptible seam" was sent to Australia. Simultaneously a higher grade woven woollen cloth had been adopted, to remain the standard pattern for many years.

To-day the ball with the stitchless cover is decreed by the International Federation and is common to all countries. Inside the ball, however, the same uniformity does not prevail. In theory a plugless ball may be superior to the ball which uses a plug for inflation purposes; in actual play there can be no appreciable difference. If a ball is dropped vertically on a concrete base, and the plug chances to be at one side rather than at the point of contact, or

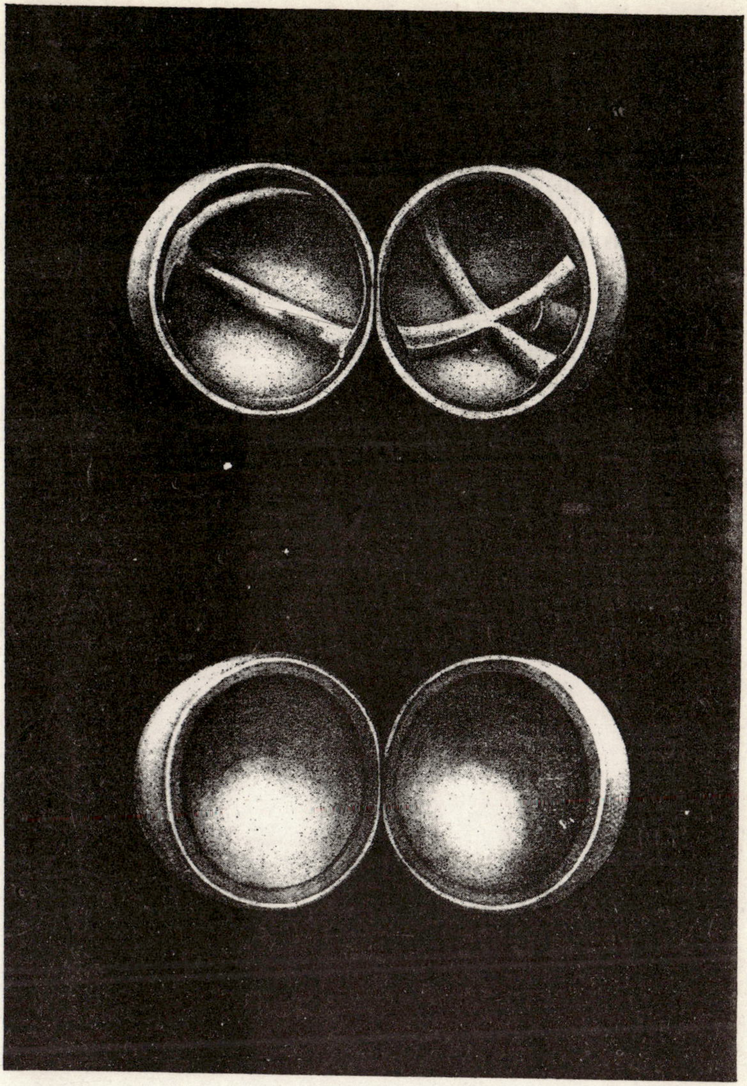

Fig. 8.

THE PLUGGED BALL.

Fig. 9.

THE PLUGLESS BALL.

immediately above the point of contact, the weight of the plug, which is less than one-twenty-eighth of an ounce, will tend to deviate it from a straight line. But when the ball has forward motion, as it always has in play, the influence of the plug is negligible.

It has often been remarked by visitors to both countries that the balls of America and Great Britain do not respond to stroke play in the same way. The physical properties of the balls used in both countries are now virtually identical, but their behaviour cannot fail to be influenced by differences in climate and soil—just as balls of the same make will bound differently on various courts in the same country. A ball on a dry court in a hot, clear atmosphere will bound not only inches but often feet higher than the same ball on a damp, soft court in a heavy, moist air. British turf, because of the climate and the character of the soil, is generally thicker and heavier than American turf; this again affects the bound. It may be doubted, however, whether the real champion, in a week or two, cannot reconcile his game to meet either conditions; the records of H. L. Doherty, R. Lacoste, W. T. Tilden, and W. M. Johnston in both hemispheres suggest that he can.

CHAPTER
SIXTEEN

THE RULES OF LAWN TENNIS

CHAPTER SIXTEEN

THE RULES OF LAWN TENNIS

The Singles Game.

1. THE Court shall be a rectangle, 78 feet long and 27 feet wide. It shall be divided across the middle by a net, suspended from a cord, or metal cable of a maximum diameter of $\frac{1}{3}$rd of an inch, the ends of which shall be attached to, or pass over, the tops of two posts, 3 feet 6 inches high, which shall stand 3 feet outside the Court on each side. The height of the net shall be 3 feet at the centre, where it shall be held down taut by a strap not more than 2 inches wide. There shall be a band covering the cord or metal cable and the top of the net for not less than 2 inches nor more than $2\frac{1}{2}$ inches in depth on each side. The lines bounding the ends and sides of the Court shall respectively be called the Baselines and the Side-lines. On each side of the net, at a distance of 21 feet from it and parallel with it, shall be drawn the Service-lines. The space on each side of the net between the service-line and the side-lines shall be divided into two equal parts called the Service-courts by the centre-service-line, which must be 2 inches in width, drawn half-way between and parallel with the side-lines. Each baseline shall be bisected by an imaginary continuation of the centre-service-line to a line 4 inches in length and 2 inches in width, called the centre-mark, drawn inside the Court, at right angles to and in contact with such baseline. All other lines shall be not less than 1 inch nor more than 2 inches in width, except the baselines, which may be 4 inches in width, and all measurements shall be made to the outside of the lines.

Note.—In the case of the International Lawn Tennis Championship (Davis Cup) or other official championships of the International Federation, there shall be a space behind each baseline of not less than 21 feet, and at the sides of not less than 12 feet.

2. The permanent fixtures of the Court shall include

not only the nets, posts, cord, or metal cable, strap, and band, but also, where there are any such, the back and side stops, the stands, fixed or movable seats and chairs round the Court, and their occupants, all other fixtures around and above the Court, and the Umpire, Foot-fault Judge, and Linesmen when in their respective places.

3. The outer surface of the ball shall be smooth and without stitches. The ball shall be more than $2\frac{1}{2}$ inches and less than $2\frac{5}{8}$ inches in diameter, and not less than 2 ounces, nor more than $2\frac{1}{16}$ ounces in weight. The ball shall have a minimum bound of 53 inches and a maximum bound of 58 inches when dropped 100 inches at a temperature approximating to 68 degrees Fahrenheit upon a concrete base, and a deformation of not less than ·290 of an inch and not more than ·315 of an inch when subjected to a pressure of 18 lb. applied to each end of any diameter at a temperature approximating to 68 degrees Fahrenheit. All tests for deformation shall be carried out in accordance with the instructions in the Appendix hereto.

4. The players shall stand on opposite sides of the net; the player who first delivers the ball shall be called the Server, and the other the Receiver.

5. The choice of sides and the right to be Server or Receiver in the first game shall be decided by toss. If the winner of the toss choose the right to be Server or Receiver, his opponent shall have the choice of sides. If the winner of the toss takes the choice of sides his opponent shall have the right to be Server or Receiver. The winner of the toss may, if he prefer it, require his opponent to make the first choice.

6. The service shall be delivered in the following manner. Immediately before commencing to serve, the Server shall stand with both feet at rest behind (*i.e.* farther from the net than) the baseline and within the imaginary continuation of the centre-mark and side-line. The Server shall then project the ball by hand into the air *in any direction* and strike it with his racket, and the delivery shall be deemed to be completed at the moment of the impact of the racket and the ball. A player with the use of only one arm may utilise his racket for the projection.

7. The Server shall throughout the delivery of the service
   (*a*) Not change his position by walking or running;
   (*b*) Maintain contact with the ground;
   (*c*) Keep both feet behind (*i.e.* farther from the net than) the baseline.

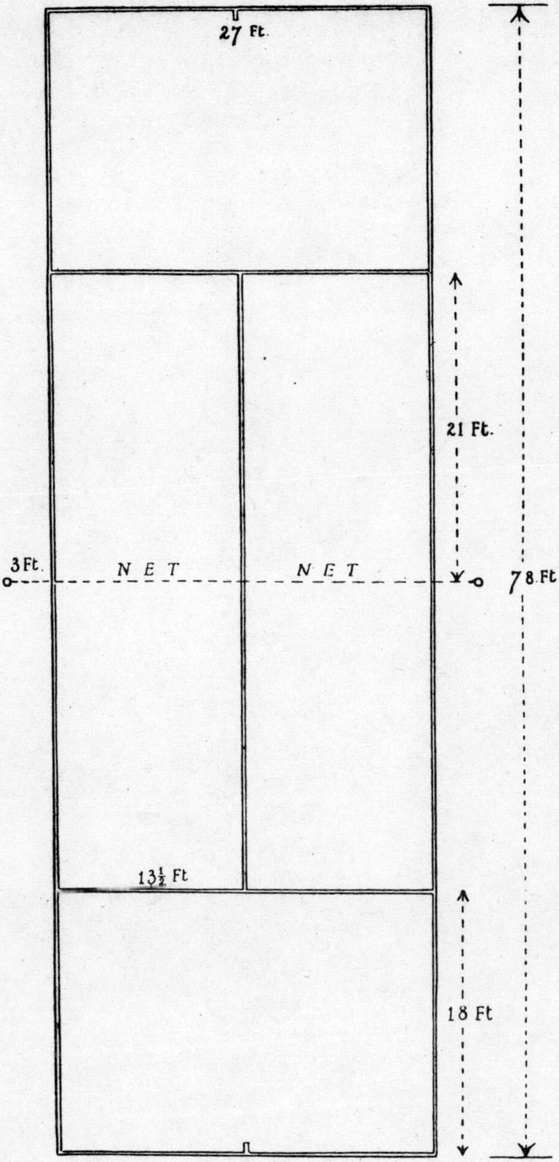

Fig. 10

SINGLES COURT.

8. In delivering the service, the Server shall stand alternately behind the right and left Courts, beginning from the right in every game. The ball served shall pass over the net and hit the ground within the Service-court which is diagonally opposite, or upon any line bounding such Court, before the Receiver returns it.

9. The service is a fault : (*a*) If the Server commit any breach of Rules 6, 7, or 8 ; (*b*) If he miss the ball in attempting to strike it ; (*c*) If the ball served touch a permanent fixture (other than the net, strap, or band) before it hits the ground.

10. After a fault (if it be the first fault) the Server shall serve again from behind the same half of the Court from which he served that fault, unless it was a fault because he served from behind the wrong half, when he shall be entitled to deliver one service from behind the other half.

A fault may not be claimed after the next service has been delivered.

11. The Server shall not serve until the Receiver is ready. If the latter attempt to return the service, he shall be deemed ready. If, however, the Receiver signify that he is not ready, he may not claim a fault because the ball does not hit the ground, within the limits fixed for the service.

12. The service is a let : (*a*) If the ball served touch the net, strap, or band, provided the same be otherwise good ; (*b*) If a service or fault be delivered when the Receiver is not ready (see Rule 11). In case of a let, the service counts for nothing, and the Server shall serve again, but a let does not annul a previous fault.

13. At the end of the first game the Receiver shall become Server, and the Server Receiver ; and so on alternately in all the subsequent games of a match. If a player serve out of turn, the player who ought to have served shall serve as soon as the mistake is discovered, but all points scored before such discovery shall be reckoned. If a game shall have been completed before such discovery, the order of the service remains as altered. A fault served before such discovery shall not be reckoned.

14. A ball is in play from the moment at which it is delivered in service (unless a fault or a let), and remains in play till the point is decided.

15. The Server wins a point : (*a*) If the ball served touch the Receiver or anything which he wears or carries before it hits the ground ; (*b*) If the Receiver otherwise lose a point as provided by Rule 17.

16. The Receiver wins the point: (*a*) If the Server serve two consecutive faults; (*b*) If the Server otherwise lose the point as provided by Rule 17.

17. A player loses the point if—

(*a*) He fail, before the ball in play has hit the ground twice consecutively to return it directly over the net [except as provided in Rule 20(*c*)]; or

(*b*) He return the ball in play so that it hits the ground, a permanent fixture, or other object outside any of the lines which bound his opponent's Court; or

(*c*) He volley the ball and fail to make a good return even when standing outside the Court; or

(*d*) He touch or strike the ball in play with his racket more than once in making a stroke; or

(*e*) He or his racket (in his hand or otherwise) or anything which he wears or carries touch the net, posts, cord or metal cable, strap or band, or the ground within his opponent's Court at any time while the ball is in play; or

(*f*) He volley the ball before it has passed the net; or

(*g*) The ball in play touch him or anything that he wears or carries, except his racket in his hand or hands; or

(*h*) He throws his racket at and hits the ball.

18. A ball falling on a line is regarded as falling in the Court bounded by that line.

19. If the ball in play touch a permanent fixture (other than the net, posts, cord or metal cable, strap or band) after it has hit the ground, the player who struck it wins the point; if before it hits the ground, his opponent wins the point.

20. It is a good return—

(*a*) If the ball touch the net, posts, cord or metal cable, strap or band, provided that it passes over any of them and hits the ground within the Court;

(*b*) If the ball, served or returned, hit the ground within the proper Court and rebound or be blown back over the net, and the player whose turn it is to strike reach over the net and play the ball, provided that neither he nor any part of his clothes or racket touch the net, posts, cord or metal cable, strap or band, or the ground within his opponent's Court, and that the stroke be otherwise good;

(*c*) If the ball be returned outside the post, either above or below the level of the top of the net, even though it touch the post, provided that it hits the ground within the proper Court ;

(*d*) If a player's racket pass over the net after he has returned the ball, provided the ball pass the net before being played and be properly returned ;

(*e*) If a player succeed in returning the ball, served or in play, which strikes a ball lying in the Court.

21. In case a player is hindered in making a stroke by anything not within his control, except a permanent fixture of the Court, the point shall be re-played.

22. If a player wins his first point, the score is called 15 for that player ; on winning his second point, the score is called 30 for that player ; on winning his third point, the score is called 40 for that player, and the fourth point won by a player is scored game for that player, except as below—

If both players have won three points, the score is called deuce ; and the next point won by a player is scored advantage for that player. If the same player wins the next point, he wins the game ; if the other player wins the next point the score is again called deuce ; and so on, until a player wins the two points immediately following the score at deuce, when the game is scored for that player.

23. The player who first wins six games wins a set, except as below :

If both players have won five games, the score is called games-all, and the next game won by a player is scored advantage game for that player. If the same player wins the next game, he wins the set ; if the other player wins the next game, the score is again called games-all ; and so on until a player wins two games more than his opponent, when the set is scored for that player.

24. The players shall change sides at the end of the first, third, and every subsequent alternate game of each side, and at the end of each set, unless the total number of games in such set be even, in which case the change is not made until the end of the first game of the next set.

25. The maximum number of sets in a match shall be five, or, where women take part, three.

26. Except where otherwise stated, every reference in these Rules to the masculine includes the feminine.

27. In matches where an Umpire is appointed, his decision shall be final ; but where a Referee is appointed an appeal shall lie to him from the decision of an Umpire on a question of law, and in all such cases the decision of the Referee shall be final.

The Referee, in his discretion, may at any time postpone a match on account of darkness or the condition of the ground or the weather. In any case of postponement the previous score and previous occupancy of courts shall hold good, unless the Referee and the players unanimously agree otherwise.

28. Play shall be continuous from the first set until the match be concluded ; provided that after the third set, or, when women take part, the second set, either player is entitled to a rest, which shall not exceed ten minutes, and provided further that when necessitated by circumstances not within the control of the players, the Umpire may suspend play for such a period as he may consider necessary. These provisions shall be strictly construed, and play shall never be suspended for the purpose of allowing a player to recover his strength or his wind. The Umpire shall be the sole judge of intentional delay, and after giving due warning he may disqualify the offender.

Note.—Any Nation is at liberty to modify the first provision of this Rule or omit it from its regulations governing tournaments, matches, or competitions held in his own country other than the International Lawn Tennis Championship (Davis Cup).

The Doubles Game.

29. The above Rules shall apply to the Doubles Game except as below.

30. For the Doubles Game, the Court shall be 36 feet in width, *i.e.* 4½ feet wider on each side than the Court for the Singles Games, and those portions of the singles side-lines which lie between the two service-lines shall be called the service side-lines. In other respects, the Court shall be similar to that described in Rule 1, but the portions of the singles side-lines between the baseline and the service-line on each side of the net may be omitted if desired.

31. The pair who have the right to serve in the first game of each set may decide which partner shall do so, and the opposing pair may decide similarly for the second

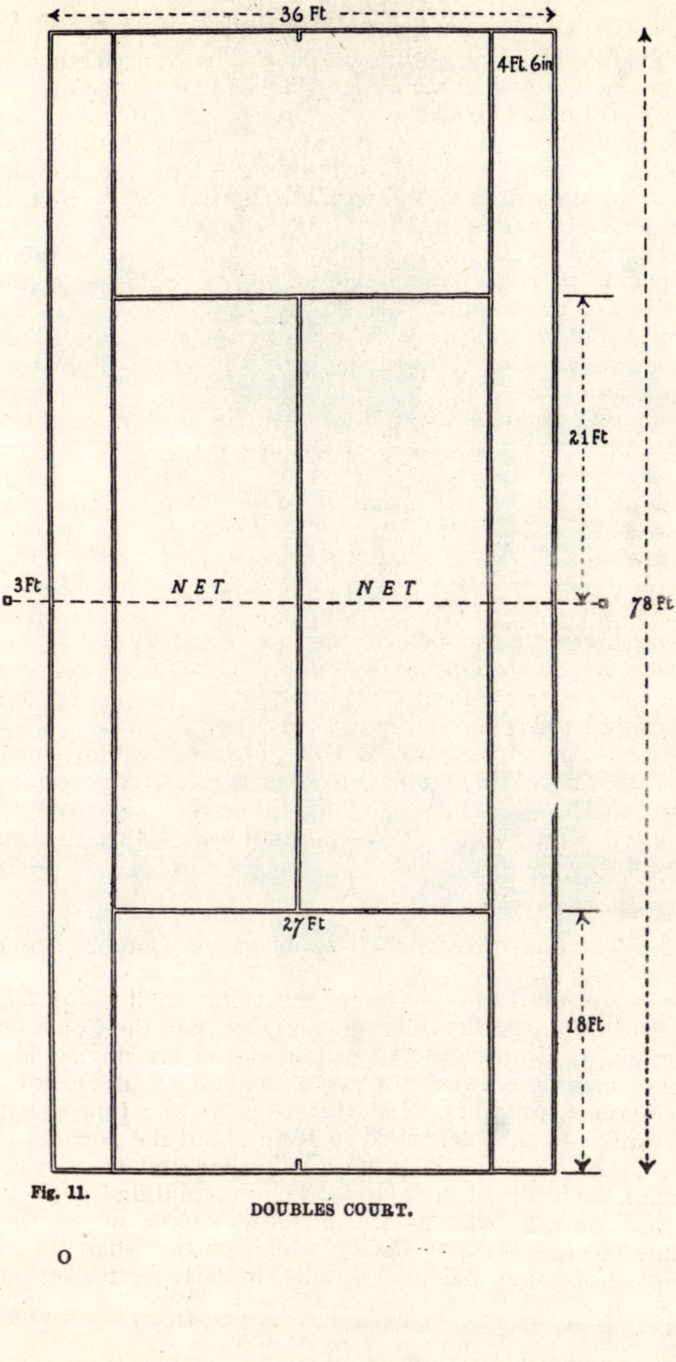

Fig. 11.

DOUBLES COURT.

O

game. The partner of the player who served in the first game shall serve in the third; the partner of the player who served in the second game shall serve in the fourth, and so on in the same order in all the subsequent games of a set.

The order of service having been arranged may not be altered during the set, but it may be changed at the beginning of each new set. Similarly, the Receivers may not change places with each other for the purpose of receiving the service before the end of a set, but they may do so at the beginning of a new set.

32. The service is a fault as provided for by Rule 9, or if the ball served touch the Server's partner or anything which he wears or carries; but if the ball served touch the partner of the Receiver or anything which he wears or carries, before it hits the ground, the Server wins the point.

33. If a partner serve out of his turn, the partner who ought to have served shall serve as soon as the mistake is discovered, but all points scored, and any fault served before such discovery, shall be reckoned. If a game shall have been completed before such discovery, the order of service remains as altered.

34. The players to receive the service shall receive it alternately throughout each game. The order thus established shall not be altered during the set.

35. The ball shall be struck alternately by one or other player of the opposing pairs, and if a player touches the ball in play with his racket in contravention of this Rule, his opponents win the point.

Appendix to Rules of Lawn Tennis.

Instructions to be followed in all Tests for "Deformation" conducted under Rule 3.

1. In all tests for deformation conducted under Rule 3, the machine designed by Percy Herbert Stevens and Patented in Great Britain under Patent No. 230,250, together with the subsequent additions and improvements thereto, shall be employed.

2. The test shall be conducted at a temperature of approximately 68 degrees Fahrenheit, and any ball to be tested shall be of that temperature throughout when the test is commenced.

3. Immediately before any ball is tested, it shall be dropped four times from a height of one hundred inches on a concrete base.

4. To ascertain the deformation of any ball, three readings shall be taken—one each of three diameters at right angles to one another—so chosen that initially neither platen of the machine shall be in contact with any part of the cover seam. The average of these three readings shall be the deformation reading.

5. After the ball has been placed in position, the contact weight applied, the beam brought to the pointer level, the pointers set at zero, and the test weight placed on the beam, the pressure shall then be applied to the ball by turning the hand wheel at a uniform speed, and exactly five seconds shall elapse from the instant the beam leaves its seat until it is brought to the pointer level, whereupon the turning shall cease and the reading shall be taken.

6. The limits specified are fixed for a test conducted in an atmospheric pressure resulting in a barometric reading of approximately 29.95.